M. A. Nannary

Memoirs of the life of Rev. E.J. Dunphy

M. A. Nannary

Memoirs of the life of Rev. E.J. Dunphy

ISBN/EAN: 9783337053864

Printed in Europe, USA, Canada, Australia, Japan

Cover: Foto ©ninafisch / pixelio.de

More available books at **www.hansebooks.com**

MEMOIRS

OF THE

LIFE

OF

Rev. E. J. Dunphy,

BY

M. A. NANNARY.

SAINT JOHN, N. B.
Printed at the Weekly Herald Job Rooms,
1877.

Introduction.

No matter how sweet or endearing the memory of those we love, Time, the destroyer of all things, will dim that memory, unless replenished by the frequent recital or perusal of the many virtues that in life so commanded the esteem and admiration of one's fellow man. How many great and noble men, now mouldering in the dust of their narrow graves, are entirely forgotten by the thousands who, even after many ages, have been benefited by their expansive intellects, and noble, unselfish lives. How many grand, sublime, and generous sacrifices have been made by millions which have never been recorded in the book of Time, while others have left after them many living monuments that continually speak to the mind and heart of the great good quietly and noiselessly accomplished during their life-time.

I do not claim for the subject of these Memoirs that he was a *great* man, great in the sense the world uses the word; but I do hold he was a good man, a faithful servant of God, a holy priest, one who fearlessly and independently did what he knew or felt to be his duty, and who, by his consistent piety and unblemished reputation, shed honor on the sacred calling of the priesthood. Great, exalted, and sublime is the mission of the true Catholic priest, raising him superior to his fellow man through the agency of that ministry, established centuries ago, and which will remain firm and undimmed till the end of time. Not even those outside of the fold of the Roman Catholic Church can look upon the priest, in some of the many situations of life, without respect for the man, and silent admiration for the religion he represents. Take, for instance, the poor fever stricken patient, or still worse, the frail man or woman smitten with some loathsome and contagious disease. Who is the first to enter fearlessly into that small contracted room, laden with its foul, pestilential air, and minister to the spiritual or temporal wants of the already perhaps forsaken father or mother, or the once dearly loved sister or brother? He is also prepared in the dead and silent watches of the night to be aroused from his sweet and much needed rest, to brave the cold and biting blasts of a dreary winter night, in order that he may bring spiritual aid and comfort to some poor child committed to his pastoral care. In the early watches of the morning he kneels before the altar of God, and earnestly, lovingly, implores His mercy in behalf of the many dear children confided to his spiritual keeping; and again, when all nature is hushed to the deepest silence, does he bow in reverential awe before that same altar, with none to hear his low murmured prayers, save the white winged angels lingering lovingly by to waft his many petitions to the throne of Love and Mercy. Quietly, silently he prays on, the dim, steady light from the altar shedding around on those no less silent, though sacred walls, its subdued and sombre rays, and for the time one forgets there is an outside world, where the fierce passions of man rage and God is hourly, nay momentarily, offended. Such is the true priest of God, mediator as it were between man and his Creator, and such was the daily, nightly life of Father Dunphy, during his pastoral charge of twenty-seven years.

Rev. E. J. Dunphy will, I am sure, be only forgotten by some when the feeble breath of life flickers in the frail, emaciated frame; but to others, who were not granted the privilege of knowing him so well, time will naturally dim, if not entirely obliterate, the memory of this good man, this holy priest. It is to keep alive this memory that I have undertaken, with many misgivings, a short and I fear very imperfect sketch of his energetic, hard-working life. I have done so at the urgent request of my many friends and his, knowing him as I did from childhood, till death closed the scene and dimmed the failing powers of one upon whom I ever looked as a true, sincere friend, a kind, affectionate father, and a most worthy and zealous pastor.

Many an old resident can tell much better than I of the energetic young priest, who entered on his Carleton mission some twenty-five years ago. How he came in their midst with his youthful, boyish face, a comparatively young man, but with a burning zeal for God's honor and glory, and an ardent desire for their spiritual and temporal welfare, more in keeping with a man of mature years and one who had long been burdened with the many cares and duties incidental to a priest's self-sacrificing life. How the parish was then in its infancy; of the material work undertaken and accomplished with so much enthusiasm, and of the still nobler and grander efforts he made for the moral, social, and intellectual improvement in the condition of the people entrusted to his watchful care. The former remain as living monuments to his zeal and energy, while the latter can only speak in the daily lives of the thousands whom he taught with unwearying patience to love God, to be good and upright citizens, true to themselves and each other, never swerving from the right, and in all things to act honestly and honorably, with an independance which made them adhere to the right and disavow all that was wrong, socially, religiously and politically. On the altar, in the confessional, or at the death-bed of some poor, dying creature, he was ever found in the conscientious discharge of his manifold duties.

In his private life he was a thorough gentleman, a princely host, and a truly reliable friend. It was in his every day life, particularly in his private devotions to God, that the real, genuine virtues of the man shone forth with a lustre which must necessarily leave a lasting impression on those who were the daily, though silent, witnesses of his truly holy and edifying life. He had, I grant, his faults and imperfections. Who has not? But over these let us draw the veil of charity, and now, that he lies among the motionless and silent dead, let us not think otherwise than kindly and lovingly of the one whose mute lips cannot speak in his own defence.

In order that an adequate idea may be given of the work accomplished during the life-time of Father Dunphy, it will, I think, be well, before introducing him personally to the notice of the reader, to commence at the very establishment of the Catholic Church in Carleton. I will, therefore, with your kind permission, diverge for a few moments from the subject of my sketch.

CHAPTER I.

Well, reader mine, will you, for an hour or so, throw aside the cares and duties of the day, and come back with me, in imagination, some thirty-one or two years ago, when together we will watch the progress of the Catholic Church in Carleton; a theme ever dear to the true Catholic heart, no matter how or where situated. Thirty-one or two years ago! It seems a very long time from which to cite memories of the past; but, with a little thought and care, we will, I am sure, bring our work to a satisfactory issue. Yes, a little more than a quarter of a century ago, there stood not one vestige of that noble church, with its chaste and elegant surroundings, which to-day proclaims with a silent, though no less eloquent tongue, the faith, piety, and undaunted perseverance of those who have, through the aid of their good priest, raised such a noble structure to the honor of that God in whom they believe and hope for eternal life. Yes, at the time of which I write, Carleton was a poor, struggling village, its inhabitants, comparatively small in number, supporting themselves by fishing and the lumber business, which had at that time but a name.

The majority of the resident population were Protestants; the Catholics then not numbering more than fifty families in all. In regard to religion they were, I may say, in an almost isolated condition—no church, no priest, and some few of them consequently forgetting, when deprived of all external forms of worship, that there was a God. At that time St. John was supplied with only one Catholic Church, which up to the memorable 20th of June of the present year bore the name of Old Saint Malachi's. Dear old Church! How can I coldly and silently pass you by without at least a friendly notice; but I fear any direct reference would be scarcely considered in keeping with my present subject. Dear old Saint Malachi's! how many fond memories, how many sweet and hallowed recollections twine around thy holy altar, as numberless Catholics remember thee during the many active years of thy existence. How many sacred and holy memories cluster around thee as thousands recollect when untouched by the world's care, they knelt for the first time within thy sacred portals. Yes! for more than half a century did Saint Malachi's Church stand firm and undisturbed amidst the various storms of wind and rain, nobly did this time-honored institution battle with the fierce and varied elements, until the fatal and eventful 20th of June, when, among many other noble and useful structures, it too fell a victim to the fiery scourge which left our fair city a sad spectacle of ruin, misery and desolation.

To this Church was attached the good and worthy Bishop Dollard, who had removed his Episcopal See from Fredericton to St. John, and two or three priests, all too little for the requirements of the people, whose numbers were weekly increasing by the many emigrants from Ireland, who were reluctantly compelled to leave the land of their birth and seek freedom and a home in this portion of vast and free America. At this place of worship the more piously inclined of the Carleton people endeavored to assist on at least occasional Sundays, being compelled to go by means of small boats, during which, on more than one occasion, the lives of all were endangered, either by the wildness of the sea or the mismanagement of those whose duty it was to propel the frail boats across our harbor. This unpleasant state of affairs continued for some time, till at last, weary of the constant annoyance, coupled with the extreme danger attending these expeditions, the people unanimously agreed among themselves to erect a Church for their own use, and which would better supply the many spiritual wants of the people of Carleton. In consequence of this resolution, a meeting was held in the house of Mr. Peter Fagan, one of the then most respected residents of the place. With written resolutions to this effect, two or three members waited on His Lordship **Bishop Dollard, and** it was with evident pleasure they retired from the worthy prelate's presence, having received the assurance from him that in all things relating to the honor of **God** and their spiritual welfare, they would have his willing assistance and hearty co-operation.

CHAPTER II.

THE FIRST CATHOLIC CHURCH IN CARLETON.

In accordance with the promise made by Bishop Dollard he lost no time in waiting on the Hon. John Robertson, who at that time, with many of the earlier settlers, held possession of an unlimited extent of land, wild and uncultivated it is true, but which proved of much value to its fortunate owners. Two acres were accordingly purchased for the comparatively trifling sum of $560. On this piece of land was commenced the first Catholic Church in 1847, which was but partly finished in 1849. The " Little Chapel," as it has been familiarly called, was only **54x60**, which gives the reader an idea of the extent of the building. Though small, it was found to be quite large enough for many years for the requirements of the Catholic community. Much cannot be written in praise of its interior or exterior beauty, being a building sadly lacking in appearance that architectural proportion which now almost invariably marks the artistic and finished workman. Rude though it may have been to the eye looking for external beauty, it was nevertheless a bright, happy morning to the humble worshippers kneeling before that altar on which was celebrated the holy sacrifice of the Mass. There, for the first time, they knelt in united prayer, and who can doubt the warmth of their grateful Irish hearts, as they thanked the Divine Victim for the unspeakable blessings of that day, and from this happy era we may date the continued rise and spread of Catholicity in Carleton.

CHAPTER III.

REV. EDMUND QUINN.

During some two or three years the people of Carleton had the occasional services of some of the priests resident in the city, which occasioned the people at times many disappointments. This was owing to the unlimited number of calls made on the services of the hard-working clergymen, who had a large city and surrounding country to attend. Much dissatisfaction being evinced, the good Bishop thought it better to send a resident priest to Carleton, who could better attend to the spiritual wants of the people. Accordingly, in 1850, Rev. Edmund Quinn took up his residence in Carleton, and to the many requirements of his people, he ministered with care, zeal and promptitude, till he was taken ill, which illness continuing he was rendered physically unfit for the further discharge of his active priestly duties. "Father Edmund," (as he was lovingly and familiarly called by his much attached congregation), with the spirit and determination characteristic of the man, attended, though ill, to the many business details of his pastoral charge, while his brother, Rev. James Quinn (now the respected pastor of St. Stephen,) celebrated Mass and assumed all the outside duties of the Parish until his departure for St. Andrews in 1852. Father Edmund continued to reside with his brother till his death, in the winter of 1874, when, let us hope, he was called to receive the reward of that patience with which he bore the intense physical suffering of so many long, weary years.

CHAPTER IV.

REV. E. J. DUNPHY.

The Parish of Carleton becoming again vacant, Bishop Connolly, the late lamented Archbishop of Halifax, who succeeded Bishop Dollard to the Episcopal See of St. John, recalled from a Parish at the North Shore, Rev. E. J. Dunphy, and appointed him Pastor of the Catholic Church in Carleton. Young, fervent, and full of zeal for the honor of that God to whom he unreservedly offered his entire life, to him is due, in an especial manner, many improvements that meet the eye of the beholder; living monuments that speak more forcibly to the mind and heart than any words of mine can ever effect.

Rev. Edward John Dunphy, the eldest son of Thomas and Honora Dunphy, was born April 14th, 1824, in the beautiful city of Waterford, Ireland, and was baptized in the Church of the Holy Trinity, by Rev. Father Burke. In 1829, he sailed from Ireland with his parents, and, arriving in New York, they, like many others of the Irish population, made their home in that populous and now widely known American city. He was then five years of age, and during a portion of the intervening years spent there he served on the altar of Saint Ann's Church. On September 12th, 1833, and consequently when only nine years old, he lost his mother, who died at the early age of thirty-two years. This was the first grief that entered into his young life, the first sorrow that pressed heavily on his youthful, boyish spirits—a grief that during his busy, hard-working career was never entirely laid aside, a sorrow that was never completely forgotten. How many, many times I heard him refer with pleasure and affection to the gentle woman who, in his lonely boyhood, had been lost to him; how bitterly he bemoaned her sudden and unexpected death; and though but a child at the time, how vivid seemed his rememberance of the day on which they carried her from the now lonely, cheerless home, made so often bright and happy by the sweet and endearing attentions of a mother's gentle, loving presence. How many, grown even to manhood and battling with the world's hard, stern realities, can look back through the vista of many years and echo the same thoughts and feelings which, during a life-time, seemed exclusively his own. Such is life. Early we begin to learn the cold, hard lesson; but no trial can be equal to the loss—particularly in early childhood—of that sustaining, unselfish love, found pure and unalloyed in the heart of a truly good and loving **mother**. How many, occupying positions of **power** and influence, look back upon the years of their fortunate childhood, and, with grateful, loving hearts, thank a mother's watchful care, who not only taught them to love and revere all that was pure and good, but at the same time instilled into their young hearts and **minds** an equal love for that manly principle which, during **all the** phases of their chequered career, made them instinctively shrink **from the** commission of the smallest act which would involve that honor, the brightest ornament of **the** truly noble mind. But I am digressing.

In 1839, six years after the loss of **his lamented** mother, Father Dunphy sailed from **New York for** St. John, reaching here after a rough and disagreeable voyage of **several days.** He came through the invitation of his uncle, Dean Dunphy, well and personally remembered **by** several in Saint John and vicinity, particularly by many now grown old, but whose memory carries them back to the first years of their residence in this city. He did not remain long with his uncle, as it was the desire **of** the latter that he should study for the Church, and **with** this intention he sent him **to** Saint Andrew's College, Prince Edward Island. There he remained three years, his course of studies embracing English, French and Latin. The Professor of the College at that time was John Slattery, a remarkably clever, but very eccentric, man, whose peculiarities and eccentricities were a constant and never wearying source of amusement to the students. He subsequently resigned his position as teacher in the College, joined a religious order some distance outside of New York, was eventually ordained priest, and again filled the position of teacher in the college attached to the order. He never discharged the active duties of the priesthood, and after many years of faithful service he passed from earth, let us hope, to a happier and better world. Among the twenty-four students in the college at the period of which I write, was our worthy Bishop, Right Rev. Dr. Sweeny; Very Rev. Thomas Connolly, Vicar General of Saint John, and the present esteemed and respected pastor of Carleton; Rev. John Mooney, who has, we trust, ere this received the reward of his short, though faithful, stewardship; Rev. James McDonald, Vicar-General of Prince Edward Island, and Rev. William McDonald, now in the United States. As a student, Father Dunphy was not particularly noticeable for any remarkable talent, many of his classmates far surpassing him in quickness and brilliancy of intellect. He was especially dull in classics, but could write with ease, and on some subjects showed much natural ability. He was at all times a close reader of books, and there still stands in front of the college door an old oak tree under which he would sit and read, never wearied of poring over the writings of some old and favorite author. In this quiet and secluded spot he was often surprised by the appearance of some favorite classmate in search of the wanderer, and here he was sure to be found during many of his leisure moments, engaged in his favorite pursuit, or mayhap dreaming, like all youthful visionaries, of the dim, uncertain future. Though not naturally brilliant, he was ambitious, and, through close, hard study and unremitting attention, he steadily gained on some of his more fortunate fellow students, so that, at the end of his course in Saint Andrew's College, he earned the well-merited encomiums of his superiors and the praises of the more generous of his classmates. Though lacking to some extent the mental calibre of some of his more brilliant companions, he was never surpassed in his warm, sincere love for God, his consistent piety, and the regularity of his daily devotions, by which he won the entire confidence of his superiors and the unfeigned admiration and respect of his fellow-students. This piety, so noticeable even in early childhood, was characteristic of the man during the many years of his busy, active life.

In the play-ground he was found to be of an

amiable, agreeable disposition, at all times evincing a strong desire for out-door exercises, of which the large and beautiful grounds surrounding the college, situated some twenty miles from Charlottetown, afforded ample opportunities. Though small, and even fragile looking, he was remarkably strong and lithe, throwing his opponent in a boyish wrestle with apparently as little trouble as if the effort did not in the least tax his physical powers. By many of his fellow-students he was considered remarkably shrewd, and several of them took a genuine pleasure in calling him "Uncle Sam," on account of his hailing from New York. This title he by no means relished, and in a spirit of retaliation was not slow to resent the hated soubriquet, by giving his tormentors some absurd and ridiculous names. He was fully capable of taking his own part, settling his own difficulties, and was generally victorious over his youthful competitors in the various sports attached to the playground. His vacations were spent on the Island, at the invitation of his dearest friend and classmate, the present esteemed Judge Reddin. Here he was entirely and thoroughly at home, forming one of the family circle, and after many years he would refer with pleasure and grateful affection to the many happy, social hours spent beneath the kind and hospitable roof of his old friend's home. So passed three years of his college life, studying, reading and playing, while his vacations were spent in fishing, hunting, or roaming the forest, his busy, active mind always occupied in an incessant round of duties, mingled with many a boyish pastime, which go to make up a student's life at college, cut off as he is from home, friends and the familiar associations of his childhood. In 1842, he returned from the Island to Saint John, where he remained till the following summer, under the care and personal supervision of Dean Dunphy, when he went to New York, and in 1843 entered Saint John's college, Fordham. Here, within the walls of this time-honored institution, which has given to the world so many great and good men, was our youthful friend, pursuing with quiet perseverance his various studies, when at the end of a year a letter from his uncle unexpectedly recalled him to Saint John. After resting a few days he found himself on his way to Quebec, where he entered the Minor Seminary, in that city, on the 9th of October, 1844. There he remained two years, devoting his time to the study of philosophy, mathematics and logic. September 18th, 1846, he entered the Grand Seminary, where he commenced his theological course, and at the end of the third year completed that education, which was to fit him for the sacred and responsible calling of the priesthood. In that, as in Saint

Andrew's college, he enjoyed the confidence of his superiors and the love and esteem of his companions, carrying with him, when he left for his future home, the earnest prayers and sincere good wishes of his many kind associates within the well remembered walls of his dear Alma Mater.

The Most Rev. E. A. Taschereau, the venerable and saintly Archbishop of Quebec, has paid him a high tribute for his quiet, unassuming piety, strict attention to the studies in which he was engaged, and a watchful adherence to the rules and discipline of the institution of which he was at that time the honored and respected President.

February 12th, 1848, he received Minor Orders, and on the following day was made Sub-Deacon. September 28th, of the same year, he became Deacon, and on June 2nd, 1849, was ordained Priest by Bishop Dollard, in Saint Malachi's Church, in the city of Saint John. Now commences the earnest, practical, life of the hard-working, energetic Priest, who faithfully wishes to discharge the many and onerous duties of his sacred calling. The freedom of college life must be abandoned; the connection of every human tie must be severed at the call of duty, and the cross taken up manfully and courageously, in imitation of the Crucified Master, in whose footsteps they above all others are expected to follow.

Such, I doubt not, were the feelings of Father Dunphy on the memorable day of his ordination, for faithfully and conscientiously, did he try to follow the example of His Divine Model. He may have occasionally erred in the opinion of a few, in the discharge of some of his priestly duties, but his warmth and vehemence in the pulpit was due more to a burning zeal for God's honor and glory, and a desire to see each individual member of his large community so live that they would at all times, as a people, command the respect of all denominations, and consequently bring honor and respect on the religion of which he himself was so true and worthy a representative.

He celebrated his first Mass in Saint Malachi's Church, and many times I heard him refer to his first sermon. He felt comparatively easy in regard to the matter till he ascended the pulpit, when, looking around on the large congregation assembled within the walls of old Saint Malachi's, he immediately, as it were, realized his position, and, growing weak, the sight eventually faded from his eyes and he fell in a deadly swoon. Kindly sympathizing hands raised him from his prostrate position, and he knew nothing more till he awoke to consciousness in the sacristy.

In the year of his ordination he was sent to Petit Rocher, Gloucester County, and when there set to work as soon as possible to re-build the presbytery, which had been destroyed by fire a very short time previous to his being appointed to the parish. His charge at the North Shore, besides Petit Rocher, comprised Belle Dune, Black Point, and during the year 1851 and part of 1852, Riviere Jacket, Dalhousie, and Campbelltown. He was in charge of this, his first parish, only two or three years, when Bishop Connolly recalled him to Saint John, and it was with the utmost reluctance he parted from his much attached congregation, for dearly, very dearly, did he love his poor French people. How often, in after years, would he refer with evident pleasure to their love and affection, the simplicity of their lives, and the genuine regret and sorrow he experienced when obliged to leave them, through the orders of his Bishop, for in the voice of his superiors he always tried to recognize the voice of God. He remained a few months at the residence of Bishop Connolly, to whom he was even up to the time of his death sincerely and devotedly attached. He was sent to Carleton in the Fall of 1852. Now, may it indeed be said, commenced the real, thorough, earnest, every-day life of this zealous priest, who willingly, like all in his holy-calling, leave behind them all human ties and pleasures, to work for God and God alone. The Carleton congregation being then only in its infancy, there was no presbytery, and

Father Dunphy was consequently compelled to seek a home among strangers. He obtained a boarding house in the home of Charles Ketchum, Esq., and for nearly two years he remained with this gentleman and his kind and estimable lady. The fact of his residing with people of another faith naturally brought him more or less in contact with persons of other denominations, who in time learned to esteem and respect him, and by this means naturally helped to diminish that prejudice existing at this period in Carleton towards Catholics and their religion. Few if any were more capable of affecting this change than the good priest referred to.

Gentlemanly, highly polished, and strictly honourable in all his transactions, he commanded, as it were, the respect of the Protestant majority for himself and his religion, and to-day, in no place in the world, will you find more harmony of feeling and more friendly intercourse than among the many denominations of Carleton. See what one man can effect, aided by the grace of God, and blessed with those qualities which mark him at all times, and under all circumstances, not only as the minister of God, but a Christian, a man and a gentleman.

CHAPTER V.

FATHER DUNPHY'S FIRST MASS IN THE CARLETON CHURCH AND SUBSEQUENT MISSION.

On November 7th, 1852, Father Dunphy celebrated his first mass in the Carleton Church, in which perhaps there was less than a hundred persons seated on rudely constructed benches, surrounding the modest but neat and simple altar. Towards the close of Mass, he preached in plain and earnest language on the "Love of God." Could anything be more appropriate, on this his first Sunday among his future flock, than to teach them the most essential of all duties—namely, love for that God to whom they owed so much, and who, in his unbounded goodness, had in reserve for them blessings of which that day they little dreamed. The Carleton mission, at this time, embraced on the Bay of Fundy, Spruce Lake, Irish Town, Musquash, Chance Harbor, Masons Bay, and Lepreaux; on the river St. John, apart from Union Point, Spurr's Cove and Short Ferry, South Bay, Nerepis Creek, Long

Reach, and **Lynch's** settlement. At the five last named **places,** Father Dunphy gave three or four missions each year till 1860, when the **Rev. Mr.** O'Regan was appointed **the future pastor,** South Bay excepted. At **the different places** on the **Bay** he continued to give the same number of missions each year till the Fall of 1862. In scanning over with the eye the almost numberless places to be **attended** to, with more or less inhabitants in each, one cannot help saying: " What an amount of work for one man to accomplish, subjected, as he must have been, to the chilling, biting frosts of many a cold and dreary winter's night, or exposed to the scorching rays of a burning sun, during our short lived New Brunswick summer? Who can tell the countless sacrifices made by the good priest for the immortal souls committed to his care? None can know but that God to whom he has so generously devoted his entire **life,** utterly forgetful, for His sake, of those sweet and endearing ties of friendship and of kindred, which so chain the heart and affections of man to the things of earth.

CHAPTER VI.

GLEBE HOUSE, PRESENTATION, ETC.

Having been boarding now nearly a year, Father Dunphy felt the pressing necessity of having a house of his own, which might more properly be termed his home. For this purpose he contracted with Mr. Theal, of Carleton, for the erection of a Presbytery on the grounds formerly purchased for the Church. Operations were commenced on the building about the middle of June, 1853, and were completed in the same month of the following year. The amount collected for the building of the Presbytery was $1229.00, which was contributed by two hundred and fifty families, residing between Lepreaux, on the Bay of Fundy, and a portion of Long Reach, on the river St. John. The grounds, at that time, surrounding the house, were wild, barren, stony, and exceedingly uninviting, and had as an uncultivated an appearance as it is possible to imagine. The male portion of the congregation, with their strong arms and willing hands, cheerfully assembled, and, by their united and persistent efforts, so changed the appearance of the adjoining grounds that it was with difficulty one could recognize it as the barren looking plot of land of a few weeks previous. Willow and other trees were planted, and, though small in the beginning, they soon gave evidence of the knowledge, care, and combined attention of their watchful cultivator.

"Works not words," it is said (and I grant with truth), prove the sincerity of our love or appreciation. Such, at least, must have been the feelings of the Carleton people, together with the surrounding districts, for in 1854 they collected among themselves $620, for which they purchased a horse and carriage, and, with mingled feelings of pride, pleasure and affection, they presented them to their already much loved Pastor, as a trifling acknowledgment of his unceasing efforts in their regard. Need I add with what feelings of pleasure and gratification they were accepted, and many years after I heard him refer with pride and evident pleasure to his first present by the Carleton Catholic community.

CHAPTER VII.

THE MORAL AND INTELLECTUAL CONDITION OF THE PEOPLE AT THIS PERIOD.

Although the people had attained much in a spiritual sense, in a few short years, through the zeal and untiring energy of their good pastor, still there was an immense amount of work to be yet accomplished, and that which appeared the most essential, and which seemed to claim his more earnest attention, was the eradication of the sale and indulgence in strong drink, which found its way into what otherwise might have been peaceful, happy homes. To the entire and utter destruction of this evil Father Dunphy put forth every effort, using all legitimate means in his power, appealing in his most earnest manner, both in public and in private, to those engaged in the business, to turn their attention to some other mode of making a living. Still more earnestly did he conjure those who were thus employed, for the sake of their immortal souls, to confine themselves to the six days of the week, as it was then too frequently the practice to desecrate our holy Sabbath by the unlimited sale of intoxicating drinks. To judge of his success in this respect it is only necessary to state that at the end of ten years, in place of eighteen taverns, there were only seven left in the parish over which he had control. This fact alone, without further comment, proves the almost miraculous success that attended the earnest and untiring efforts of Carleton's energetic Pastor for the moral and spiritual welfare of his people. As to the means for acquiring intellectual attainments they were, indeed, quite meagre. Few, if any, schools of note were established at this time in Carleton, and these were taught by Protestant gentlemen, with now and then a Catholic teacher. With these limited educational facilities it is very evident that much had to be gained before a superior or even medium standard of intellectual acquirements could be attained.

CHAPTER VIII.

SEASON OF THE CHOLERA.

It was in this year, 1854, that the much dreaded and fatal disease of cholera burst upon St. John, with all its attendant horrors, invading peaceful, happy homes with its foul pestilential breath, tearing from thence many of its most cherished inmates, spreading death and destruction in its track, casting so much gloom and sadness among the inhabitants, bringing death to hundreds, and filling the hearts of all with well deserved fear and alarm for their own safety and preservation. How many tales of a sad and melancholy nature might be written in connection with the course of this fell destroyer throughout the city; of brother deserting brother; wives sometimes leaving their husbands, terror stricken; of homeless wanderers—waifs upon the sea of life—summarily ejected from their boarding or lodging houses, left to take care of themselves, until death put an end to their sufferings in this cold, and selfish world, hurried off to fill a rudely constructed and unknown grave, "sleeping the sleep that knows no waking," many of them far away from the friends of their youth and the once happy homes of their childhood. Carleton being in such close proximity to the city, fears were entertained that the foul contagion would be communicated to this side of the harbour, but, through the mercy of God and the earnest prayers of our saintly Pastor, the fearful and much dreaded calamity was averted. With the exception of three or four cases, Carleton was happily spared the appalling fate of being a witness of some of the terrible scenes that caused so much sorrow and distress in St. John and Portland. What a signal favour of the mercy of God in our behalf, for when we, after a lapse of twenty-three years, recall the sad and heart-rending scenes that transpired during that dreadful time, in which so many alone and entirely forsaken by human aid or comfort, were compelled to feel and witness, we should indeed be thankful for so merciful a deliverance in our regard, though perhaps in many instances less deserving than many, many hundreds who, in the full bloom of youth and manhood, were stricken down, and hurried away, to be enclosed within half made graves.

CHAPTER IX.

PEWS, PASTOR'S SALARY AND FIRST CATHOLIC CHOIR.

During the summer of 1854, pews were erected in the Church, which not only added to the appearance of the simple and modest little structure, but to the comfort of the congregation. The annual revenue derived from this source was $740.00. Previous to this year the priest's support was derived solely from the voluntary contributions of the people, but in some remarks addressed to the parishioners by Bishop Connolly he informed those present that for the future the entire revenue of the Church was to be devoted to the maintenance of the priest in charge of the parish, except that portion reserved for the requirements of the altar. This regulation gave Father Dunphy increased facilities for the further accomplishment of much good, and which always claimed his more earnest attention, particularly when relating to the beautifying or adornment of the Sacred Altar of God. It was during this year that the first Catholic Choir was formed in

Carleton, composed principally of Margaret Sullivan, Catherine Mullally, Margaret Noonan, William Mullally and James McCaffrey, none of whom at the present writing fill that honored position, being disbanded or scattered by the circumstances of life, over which we have apparently no control. The first mass sung by these ladies and gentlemen was the "Royal Gregorian Chant," a sacred composition, containing many musical beauties, which was rendered with far more credit and ability than could have been naturally expected under similar circumstances. Since that time the Choir has undergone many changes in regard to teachers and members, but an unlooked for amount of proficiency and musical knowledge was attained in a few years, and at one period it bore the enviable reputation of being the best Church Choir in the Province, with the exception of the Cathedral Choir, which was at that time under the control of the well known Coleman family.

CHAPTER X.

IMPROVEMENTS ON THE CHURCH AND THE ERECTION OF THE BELL.

In the following year, 1855, some endeavours were made to give the Church a more finished and architectural appearance if possible. For this purpose skilful and competent workmen were employed, and a tower, more in accordance with the curtailed proportions of the building, was raised on the end of the Church looking towards the Bay. It was neatly executed, and ornamented with pinnacles and other light carved wooden work, as the fancy of the good priest dictated, who had an eye for the beautiful in everything he undertook. This work proved to be quite a pleasing addition, giving a more finished and artistic look to the exterior of the building. Before completing these improvements a Bell was placed in the tower of the Church, that would, in future, summon the people to prayer. The cost of these combined improvements amounted to about $855. To raise this sum was a matter of no little consideration, but as nothing, even to the raising of money for Church purposes, can be done without a grand effort, an unusual and at that time novel means was resorted to in this instance, and that was the holding of the first pic-nic in Carleton. The words pic-nic have become as familiar now-a-days as if they had been an established law or amusement, but such has not been the case, as Father Dunphy was the first person in St. John who ever held or undertook anything of the kind, and it was to this then novel means that he resorted for the payment of the amount referred to above, There is an old, though not very elegant, expression, "Nothing venture, nothing have," and it was with feelings expressive of these words that Rev. E. J. Dunphy announced through the papers "A Grand Pic Nic for the 15th of August." The novelty of the affair would, no doubt, bring many, but whether it would be a success financially remained to be told. The much talked of pic-nic was to be held on the well known grounds of Timothy McCarthy, Esq., the scene of many a gay and festive gathering, and if ever the weather proved propitious for an undertaking of the kind, it was on that memorable 15th of August. The day was gloriously fine, the sun shining forth in all its resplendent brilliancy, and nothing could have been more inviting to the care-worn man of business, than a quiet chat, surrounded by warm and genial friends, under the cool and refreshing shade of the many trees scattered here and there around the ample grounds. Nobly, generously, did the people of Saint John respond to the general invitation extended them, and it was to the greatness of their numbers that the success of the enterprise was mainly due. Pic-nics of late years have become so frequent that it would be a superfluous and tiresome task to recount the proceedings of the day. I will only simply add that the first pic-nic held in Carleton was a complete success, financially and otherwise, giving the persevering and energetic priest, who brought the affair to so satisfactory and successful an issue, sufficient means to defray the expenses incurred during the summer. Before closing these remarks, it may not be inappropriate to add that, though these pic-nics have become a portion of our usual summer amusements, all are willing to agree that Father Dunphy's pic-nic, when held, was the picnic of the season, not solely on account of its numbers, but to the entire and total absence of all drinking and rowdyism, which but too often bring disgrace and annoyance to those closely connected with such affairs.

CHAPTER XI.

THE CATHOLIC SCHOOLS OF CARLETON.

The Schools of Catholics being so closely connected with their Church, I feel that something would be wanting to my efforts did I omit to make particular mention of the Carleton Catholic Schools and Teachers, since the opening of the first thoroughly Catholic establishment to the present time. In 1855, there was secured, by petition to the Common Council, two lots fronting each fifty feet on St. John street, and in the following year there was also purchased at auction, through G. Beatteay, Esq., two lots on George street. The annual rent of these lots was subsequently reduced by petition to the Common Council, and in 1868 another lot was secured adjoining those already purchased. Father Dunphy was particularly fortunate in procuring at reduced rents, and in a healthy, pleasant locality, suitable building accommodation, having now through his energy and perseverance secured sufficient room on which to erect a large and commodious school house, a house for the Sisters of Charity, together with ample room for a large play ground surrounding the school. Previous to this a day school had been held in the sacristy of the Church, presided over by Mr. John Finan, but the accommodations becoming too limited for the number of children wishing to gain admittance to what was then termed the "Chapel School," measures were immediately taken, after having secured the building lots, to erect a school house sufficiently large to meet the increasing demands of the promising youthful population. Accordingly a suitable building was commenced in the early part of 1856, and was completed in December of the same year, at an expenditure of $1600.00. Regular day school was commenced in January 1857, the boys being placed under the care of Mr. William Keane, the girls having for their teacher Miss Early, who has since become distinguished, being no less a personage than the famous "Cousin May Carleton," the renowned and gifted authoress, whose literary productions have been read by thousands in both hemispheres. In 1857 the upper department, or that intended for the girls, not being entirely completed, it was thought better that the boys and girls should occupy the same room in the lower portion of the building until the following spring. This department being finished and furnished in May the female pupils were removed to that part designed for their especial use. The attendance in both departments was very large, and so much anxiety was manifested by those attending to acquire that knowledge so requisite for attaining an honorable position in the mercantile world, that a night school was opened for the especial use and benefit of the young men, whose ambitious thirst for knowledge could not, owing to the nature of their pursuits, be sufficiently satisfied during the day. This school was also presided over by the hard-working and gentlemanly teacher, Mr. Keane. Affairs continued in this prosperous condition, under the first appointed teachers, till Mr. Keane, wishing to fill a position in St. Stephen, took his departure for that place, and was succeeded by Mr. Donovan. Truly may it be said, " Man proposes, but God more wisely disposes of the events surrounding the lives of his creatures." Mr. Keane bade farewell to his wife and little ones, full of the hope of sending for them in a short time ; but alas ! who can tell the future. He had scarcely reached St. Stephen when he was taken suddenly ill, and in a few short days breathed his last among strangers, having been suddenly stricken with that most loathsome of all diseases—small pox. Quickly as possible was the news communicated to Carleton, and none heard the sad intelligence without much sorrow and many regrets; sorrow for the poor young widow and her helpless orphans, so suddenly bereft of a kind husband and an affectionate father; regrets for himself, for in all his transactions with priest and people he ever proved himself that which he was, a finished scholar and a refined gentleman. Quietly he sleeps that long last sleep, surrounded by the stranger forms of many in the St. Stephen Cemetery, and while his body lies there quiet and undisturbed, let us hope that, having always lived a good life, his soul enjoys that pure and unalloyed happiness only to be found in the bosom of its Creator. I will simply refer in a few words to the Boys' School, and then, with the readers kind permission, pass on to the more interesting portion of our school history, which will, in an especial manner, relate to the female department. The male portion of our schools has been since its first establishment well and largely attended, and has in turn been ably presided over by Mr. Donovan, the successor of Mr. Keane, and for the past eight years by Mr. Thomas O'Rielly, assisted by Miss Nannary, Miss Carlind and Miss Duffy. 1872 finds the Catholics of Carleton opening their male departments under the new School Law. Satisfactory arrangements being effected between the School Trustees of the City of St. John and Father Dunphy, operations were commenced under the new law in January, and that at no compromise of honor, religion, or principle. Some time subsequent to this period the schools of Union Point, Spurr Cove and Pleasant Point, came under the same regulations, which are also in a very creditable condition—the former being satisfactorily conducted by Mr. McBrearty, assisted by Mrs. Chappell. Spurr Cove school is ably presided over by Mr. McGowan, aided by Miss Maher, while the pupils of Pleasant Point find in Miss Hamilton a very efficient teacher. Having given as satisfactory an account of the Boys' School as it is possible in these limited pages I will now turn my more particular attention to the female department. Miss Early continued her arduous duties till wearied of the monotonous routine of teaching she retired from the situation to engage in a no less arduous but much more lucrative calling. Since that time she has been occupied more or less in writing works of fiction which have been well received in the world of literature. She was replaced by Miss Margaret McCormick, a native of Prince Edward Island, and after a lapse of a few months her position was filled by her sister Harriet. These ladies taught with much success, and during the two or three years they were thus engaged succeeded in bringing the school up to a high social and intellectual standard. Miss McCormick's place was subsequently supplied by Miss Maggie Sullivan, a resident of Carleton, a pupil of the Provincial Training School, and a young lady of pleasing manners and high intellectual attainments. She was only some nine months in charge of the Carleton School, when in the fall of 1862 she was called to St. Stephen by Rev. E. J. Dunphy. She taught the St. Stephen School with much credit and ability for a year and a half, when she was taken ill, from the effects of which she never recovered, and strange to say she too reposes in peace in the St. Stephen Cemetery. She was young, talented, and much loved, particularly by the kind father and friend, who had watched in an especial manner her every step from childhood till the time when death robbed him of his much loved foster child. By the affectionate thoughtfulness of her pupils a fitting monument marks the place where reposes the form of their esteemed and kind instructor, while the flowers which are planted on her grave speak in silent though eloquent language of the warm true affection that prompted the offering. After the departure of Miss Sullivan from Carleton, Miss McCormick returned from the Island, and in turn Miss Harrigan and Miss Ferry took charge of the school, which appointments they filled with much success and ability till 1868, when the good Sisters of Charity took possession of the school. A year or two previous to this an addition had been made (by Father Quinn) to the school house, making it one of the largest and most commodious buildings of the kind in the Province. From this period may be dated the very noticeable change in the condition of the children of Carleton. Page after page of well merited praise has been written concerning the Sisters of Charity over the entire civilized world, by men and women of superior minds and extensive knowledge, and for me, with my feeble pen, to attempt to do justice to the vast amount of good annually done by these noble, self-sacrificing women, would probably result in a painful failure. In connection with a thorough practical education they have Sisters in the Convent who devote their time and abilities to the musical education of the children of those parents who are willing and able to furnish their daughters with this very desirable accomplishment. During the past three years, previous to their summer vacation, it has been usual for the Sisters to have annual exhibitions, which have been highly pleasing to those fortunate enough to be present, and which, moreover, have been received with hearty and sincere commendation by the press. The following, taken from the *Globe* of July 13th, 1871, will show the standing of these schools at that period:

"The annual exhibition of these schools took place on Thursday afternoon, and was in every respect a most pleasing and creditable entertainment. The two rooms on the ground floor were thrown into one, at the end of which were erected a stage and dressing room. His Lordship the Bishop of St. John and the Catholic priests of the city were present and a large number of visitors, probably not less than two hundred, chiefly friends and parents of the pupils. The proceedings opened with the Overture from William Tell, played by Miss Toomey and Miss Watters in capital style. Miss Collins, one of the younger pupils, then read very pleasingly, and with perfect self-possession, an affectionate address to the Bishop, who until this had not been able to attend any of the exhibitions since the Sisters of Charity took charge of the Girls' School. This was followed by an address by Miss Hanlon, after which came a drama, prepared especially for the occasion, in which six young ladies took part; an address read by Miss Rossiter; a drama, in two parts, entitled "The Two Crowns," in which Miss Muldoon, Miss Laphan, Miss Collins, Miss Toomey, Miss McCaffrey, and a number of others, acquitted themselves admirably, notwithstanding the bashfulness of some and the timidity of all. The recitation, "The Healing of the Leper," by Miss Muldoon, was very pleasing, and a dialogue on the subject of "Novel Reading" was particularly good. In this a young lad named Walshe quite distinguished himself by his fine reading of some rather lengthy speeches. Miss Kate Skerry recited "The Words of Our Lord" in a manner pleasing if not artistic. The "Rebellion" was an amusing little drama, in which the ladies of Young America, sadly aggrieved by the tyranny of old fogies, who would not give them all their own way, planned a revolt. The "Rivals" was also an agreeable school drama, in which a number of the pupils took part. After each address or dialogue there was music by Miss Toomy, Miss Collins, Miss McCaffrey, the Misses Laphan, Miss Rossiter, Miss Carroll and others. The older girls play very well, but it was almost astonishing to hear how very well some of the very little girls played. The programme was very long, but every part was well sustained throughout, and it was pleasant to hear how beautifully many of the girls read; with what correctness of emphasis, inflection and pause, and with what expression and feeling. Many, too, showed dramatic powers of no mean order, and most unconsciously rendered some telling passages in such a way as to win hearty applause from the visitors. At the close of the entertainment the Bishop addressed the pupils, thanking them for the addresses they had **read** to him, telling them how much gratification they had afforded him by the proofs of proficiency and **high** culture they had given, and paid a well merited compliment to their zealous and indefatigable pastor, **the** Rev. Mr. Dunphy. He dwelt upon **the importance of basing** all education upon religion; and **exhorted** them to show by their conduct while at school **and in their** after life, by living as good Catholics and good citizens, that they were deserving of the great opportunities this school afforded them. Rev. Mr. Dunphy also spoke. He told the pupils they had surpassed his expectations by the manner in which they had acquitted themselves. Exhibitions such as this were **he** believed the best means of teaching them how to read properly, and this is of much importance. He would tell **the** visitors, however, that reading was not the only branch taught thoroughly in the school. Arithmetic, Grammar, Natural Philosophy, and other branches, are taught with equal care, and although the children are not perpetually lectured about religion yet the education is essentially religious. Even their amusements they are taught to refer to God, and at every moment they are taught almost unconsciously **to** know and observe God's Holy Law. **He** was happy **to** be able to say that the attendance of Protestant children **at** the schools is large, usually one-seventh of **the** whole, and although the education is religious their religious feelings are never offended, their convictions never assailed in any way, and **were it** not that the teachers wear the garb of the Sisters of Charity, they might almost forget the school is Catholic. Mr. Ellis, of the *Globe*, on behalf of the visitors, expressed the gratification the exhibition afforded them. Whatever may **be** the opinions respecting denominational schools, **all the** people of Carleton admired this institution for **the great** benefits it had conferred on the whole community. **Year** after year, while he has **been a** resident of **Carleton**, he has observed the Rev. Mr Dunphy raising his **people to a** higher intellectual level, as proved by **these annual** exhibitions, and by the character of the many **rising young men** whom he had prepared to take an honourable **position** in the community He often had a hard road to **travel**, but his industry and persistent zeal overcame all **difficulties."**

Too much cannot be said in praise of the order, discipline and regularity **with** which these departments are conducted. In closing these remarks concerning the Convent Schools of Carleton, let **us hope** that years hence may be felt the good and **salutary** effects of the many earnest exhortations **which daily** issue from the lips of the hard working **Sisters of** Charity in Carleton.

In their arduous every day work the teachers of Carleton, both lay and religious, were materially aided by the watchful care and daily supervision of Father Dunphy, whose interest always centred in **the** children of his parish. Outside of his Church his Schools seemed at all times to occupy his most earnest thought and consideration, and consequently no means were left untried, no new improvement carelessly rejected, that could in any way arouse the interest in the young mind, or tend to the daily improvement and intellectual advancement of the many children under his immediate control. His own pure, child-like nature, made this duty especially pleasing to him, and I doubt not but the happiest moments of his weary, hard working life, were spent in the midst of the children in whose spiritual and temporal welfare he took so lively an interest. Yes, even as their companion in the playground, he for their sakes made himself alike unto them and entered into their childish sports with as much interest and playfulness as if he were himself a boy let loose from the unwilling restraints of the too often hated school-room. These pages will no doubt meet the eye of many a one now grown to manhood, who will recall, with mingled feelings of pleasure and sorrow, the many childish sports in which he joined, and the almost boyish pride he exhibited when unanimously proclaimed the winner in the various games. He loved all committed to his care, but, like his Divine Master, his more especial love and interest centred in "the little children," in whose pure lives and innocent faces he saw the reflection of all that was pure and good on earth.

Since April of the present year the schools of the Sisters of Charity in St. John, Portland and

Carleton, together with those taught by the Christian Brothers, have, through the liberality of the School Trustees of the city of St. John and Portland, come under the same regulations which have been in existence in the Boys' School, Carleton, since 1872, and need I add that the same harmony and good feeling which have been for the past five years characteristic of this school is now happily shared in by the several departments on either side of the river, which have so recently come under the immediate control of the Board of School Trustees of the city of St. John and Portland.

CHAPTER XII.

THE CATHOLIC LITERARY AND BAND SOCIETIES OF CARLETON.

In 1860 a Literary Society, composed principally of young men, was formed, and we all know, by either experience or observation, what an incalculable amount of good such associations do in a community. The one to which I refer is not now in existence, though I feel confident that the good arising from it is still felt by many of its existing members, for by such means young men learn in a general way much that fits them for the actual battle of life. There was considerable talent evinced by many of the young gentlemen who composed that pioneer organization, and in a couple of winters after the formation of it they produced in a highly creditable manner the chaste and classically written little religious drama, by his Eminence Cardinal Wiseman, entitled "The Hidden Gem," which was a source of pleasure to their friends and pastor, while it materially helped to swell the funds of the Society of St. Vincent de Paul, from which source many of the poor people of the parish received substantial aid and comfort during a long and dreary winter. In the same year was also formed a Brass Band, which had attained a fair proficiency, when, owing to the departure of some of its most prominent members, it was for a time disbanded, when after a lapse of some two years a second Band was reorganized, which is at the present writing in a most flourishing and prosperous condition. The members have purchased, at a cost of $520, a full and beautiful set of instruments, and in this praiseworthy and very laudable undertaking they should and I feel satisfied will receive the encouragement they so richly deserve. In fact, judging from the crowded house of January 30th, when the members, assisted by some ladies and gentlemen from Carleton and Saint John, gave their fourth annual entertainment, one could not but feel that their perseverance was warmly appreciated by their many friends and admirers, who testified their evident pleasure and desire of encouragement by giving the members a well-filled house on the occasion of their last pleasing and successful entertainment. All success then to the Carleton Serenade Band, and may it continue to flourish is, I am sure, the wish of all who have listened, with mingled feelings of pride and pleasure, to the delicious strains of harmony as they have been wafted on the balmy summer air of our quiet and unpretending Carleton.

CHAPTER XIII.

THE MUSQUASH CHURCH.

In 1858 there was purchased at Musquash, by Father Dunphy, a small tract of land, a portion of which was intended for a Cemetery, and the other on which to erect a Church. That little Church, from Carleton sixteen miles distant, was commenced in 1858 and completed in the following year. It is a pretty little structure, small and neat, but quite large enough for the requirements of the limited congregation, who are justly **proud** of their cosy little Church, and who warmly appreciated the ruling spirit who was only too happy in aiding them to such facilities for their spiritual welfare. It was constructed **at an** expenditure of $1000, and stands silently forth as another monument to the untiring zeal and energy of a good and noble priest, who, alas! is now no more.

CHAPTER XIV.

INTERIOR IMPROVEMENTS OF **THE** CHURCH.

Not being at all satisfied with the interior of his "Little Church," Father Dunphy **conceived the** idea of frescoeing, painting, and otherwise ornamenting the interior, by which **means** it would be more in accordance with his own fastidious taste and the desire of the people. For this purpose Mr. Swift was engaged, an artist who had achieved a splendid reputation, and a person highly competent to complete the work assigned him in a finished and artistic manner. The old altar was removed with the tabernacle and all its surroundings, which were replaced **by** something lighter and more pleasing to the eye. The **new** altar was purely Gothic, very florid, and beautifully illuminated, yet chaste and strictly architectural withal. In various niches of the altar there were five large figures of the Virgin and other saints. The ceiling was richly panelled with heavy mouldings in bold relief, and the ceiling of the nave was divided into eight compartments. Four of these contained groups of figures representing various scenes in the life of the Saviour, from the adoration of the Magi to the Ascension. The other four represented the most remarkable passages in the life of the Virgin. The ceilings under the galleries were panelled, and their compartments were scrolls and monograms. A new and beautiful painting was enclosed between the framework supporting the canopies that overhung the altar. It was a copy of Reuben's beautiful "Descent from the Cross," and was a gift to the Church by its zealous and progressive pastor. The Church, which was so beautifully improved and tastefully ornamented at a cost of $1155, was unanimously proclaimed by all who saw it a perfect little gem. The Church was finished in the spring of 1862, and in the fall of that year he who had done so much to make the Carleton Church and people what they were was removed to the parish of St. Stephen.

CHAPTER XV.

REMOVAL TO ST. STEPHEN.

Here for the first time in my little narrative do I pause and almost regret that I commenced these Memoirs feeling as I do my inability to do anything like adequate justice to the present Chapter. The better portion of fifteen years have passed away since the events herein recorded have taken place, but neither time nor the events incident to that period in one's life has had power to dim the saddening recollections of the fall of 1862. Truthfully, sincerely may I say, never was priest more beloved by a people than Father Dunphy was by the congregation of Carleton, and need I add deservedly so, for gratitude alone should make them feel all that warm, genuine love which the Irish people entertain, no matter how or where situated, for their dear "Sogarth Aroon." Warmly beloved as friend and pastor by every member of his congregation, the news fell upon the hearts of all like some terrible blow that leaves a weary, desolate feeling, which time alone, combined with patient resignation to the will of God, can heal. When the news of his intended departure was first circulated there were many who refused to believe it, thinking that such a thing could not be possible, that the story was without foundation, etc., etc. The strange intelligence was, however, confirmed on the following Sunday, when Father Dunphy communicated the fact from the altar, with evident emotion and regret. There are times when words are a poor exponent of one's feelings, times when our cold English language fails to convey in the most remote degree the grief and sadness of the human heart. Such in this instance were the feelings of very many, when particularly they brought up memories of the past—that past that was to them associated with that true fatherly care which made the name of Father Dunphy a treasured household word, even when time and distance intervened between him and his much loved people. The fact of his intended departure having been officially announced, proper steps were immediately taken by several members of his congregation to present him, ere he took his departure, a token of love and regret so generally felt and expressed. I will allow the address and the reply to speak for themselves, of which the following are correct copies as published in the *Freeman* of October 27th, 1862:

ADDRESS AND PRESENTATION OF THE PARISHIONERS OF CARLETON, ST. JOHN, TO THEIR BELOVED PASTOR, REV. EDWARD J. DUNPHY, PREVIOUS TO HIS LEAVING THE PARISH.

Reverend Father,—

With feelings of deep regret we meet on this day, to bid you, our dear and beloved pastor, farewell. Your departure is to us a source of much pain and sorrow, for under God we owe you many obligations. It has been your constant aim and highest ambition to make us a religious, moral, and temperate people. That, with the grace of God and by your truly Christian teaching, you have in a great measure accomplished.

What you have done for religion, for the glory of God, and our spiritual and temporal happiness, since your advent to this parish, is fully known only to God, yet it has excited the admiration of all classes in this community, as well as throughout the length and breadth of the entire **Province**.

In all your labours it seemed as if the hand of God had been aiding you, for everything prospered, everything flourished under your directing power. The respectable position we occupy, as good Catholics and good citizens, testify to you the happy fruits of your unwearied zeal and assiduity for our welfare. You have set before us the good example, by your saintly life of self denial, patience and humility,

By your indefatigable and superhuman exertions in the advocacy of the cause of temperance you have made many a household comfortable, happy and contented, which had been desolate and wretched by intemperance.

Not only for our spiritual and temporal welfare have you strenuously labored, but for that of our rising generation. With solicitude you have watched their growing and tender years, you have given them a moral and religious instruction ; in everything pertaining to their educational requirements, religious and secular, you have taken the deepest interest.

Under your benign and fostering hand the distressed, the widow, and the orphan, have found a kind father and benefactor,

Reverend Father,—We are confident that it **will give you** no little consolation to **know that** our brethren of the different denominations of Carleton and its vicinity must regret your removal, as they and you have always lived on the most friendly terms of intimacy, and you are aware that the best of good feeling has existed between them and **us for years**.

In your private sphere of life your conduct has been affable, kind and courteous to all who had the pleasing satisfaction of your acquaintance, which has distinguished you as a gentleman **composed of** the finest sensibilities.

You leave us our beautiful Church, school house and pastoral residence, as splendid monuments of your zeal and energy, the admiration **of all who** behold them, and by your good government free from debt.

Reverend and Dear Father,—As **a** token **of** our gratitude and affection for your many amiable qualities, and for all you have done for us, we present to you this purse, with its contents, of $200, being but an humble tribute to your much merited worth. May it tell you how much we love you and grieve **at your** departure.

We sincerely hope that your labors in that part of Christ's vineyard to which you are called may be as successful as they have been amongst **us**. It is our strong conviction they will, for where you are there will be order and progress in all things, spiritual **as** well as temporal. We fervently pray for your health and happiness in this life and **an** everlasting reward of felicity in the **next**. In return we ask of you, our dear Father in Christ, to remember us in your prayers.

Reverend and Dear Father,—We once more bid you farewell, and receive our assurances that your memory will always remain fresh in our hearts.

Signed in behalf of the Parishoners,

Robert Rossiter,	Felix McManus,
Timothy Nannary,	**Thos. Murphy**, Senr.,
Humphrey Toomey,	John Morris,
Richard Fitzgerald,	D. Gillis,
Michael Donovan,	William O'Hare,
Bernard Early,	T. Foley,
Terence O'Brien,	

William Nannary,
Sec. to Committee.

October 26th, 1862.

REPLY.

My Dear and Affectionate Friends :—

Words cannot possibly express the sentiments which now fill my heart. They are known but to God. Being I may say your first pastor, having passed nigh one-third of my life among you, beholding here before me hundreds that I have baptized, and of all those now before me full one-half have grown up under my spiritual care, need I say that to part with you is the saddest event of my life. The attachment, the fidelity which you have always shown me, the grief which you now manifest at my departure, your generosity on this as on many past occasions, completely overwhelm me and make me feel that, however much I may have done for you during the past ten years, I have not done one tithe enough for so good, so noble, so generous a people. But, my dear friends, my daily prayers to God has been that I might do His will on earth as it is done in Heaven; that He would make known to me the way in which I should walk and give me grace to walk therein, and I have always endeavored to consider the will of my superior as the will of God, therefore, knowing that " obedience is better than sacrifice," do I most cheerfully obey, fully convinced that whither God sends me there and only there can I be happy. And though I desire not, and never expect, greater earthly happiness than I have enjoyed in your midst, yet there are in the ways of Providence secrets that are to us impenetrable and that we shall not discover till the day of general manifestation, when the Heavens and the Earth shall proclaim that "God is just and that His ways are replete with wisdom," therefore do I feel satisfied that, were we permitted to penetrate these secrets, our mutual regrets would be changed into acts of thanksgiving, and we would bless Providence that His ways are not our ways.

In parting with you, my dear people, to labor elsewhere in God's vineyard, it is to me an immense consolation to be told by the hundreds now before me that I have deserved your esteem and love, also to be assured by our worthy Bishop that he admires and is highly pleased with the success that has attended all my labors. Yet, my dear friends, I feel that I am undeserving of all the praise you have lavished on me, and that to your generosity and promptness to comply with all my requests is due a large share of whatever success may have attended my labors. True I have always had your eternal and temporal welfare most sincerely at heart. I have laboured to the best of my humble abilities to make you true and fervent servants of God; I have had a burning thirst to see you lead edifying and irreproachable lives; I have heartily grieved when you were guilty of any act that tended to bring odium upon your religion, your country, or yourselves; in a word, my entire happiness has been wound up with yours so that I rejoiced when you were happy and was sorrowful when you were sad. This, indeed, is all true; but were I devoid of those feelings I would be an unworthy pastor, a contemptible hireling. I however deeply appreciate your affectionate address and am sincerely grateful for your munificent present. Often during the past ten years have you given me abundant mementoes of your generosity and affectionate regards, full one thousand dollars have you already presented to me in a similar manner, yet, rest assured, that far more than those perishable mementoes do I prize those tears that you shed, those sobs that you heave at my departure.

As to the efforts that I have made to eradicate intemperance from among you and make you a temperate people in this I truly find, and am happy to perceive that my efforts have not been in vain, that a love of temperance and a disgust for intemperance is daily increasing among you. God grant that it may continue to augment and that I may have the consolation of always hearing of you that which my heart so much desires, that you are models of sobriety and temperance, for to the abuse of these virtues may be traced all your misfortunes and mishaps. Abhor then my dear people a vice so fertile in misfortune and so deserving of God's wrath. I am indeed delighted to know that my removal is much regretted by the Protestants of this community, and that so good a feeling exists between you and them,—may it be ever so. Ten years ago Carleton was the hotbed, the very focus of Orangeism, and as a necessary result man hated his fellow man. That curse has disappeared from among us, and behold we now live together, not as the carnal Jews, who believed in an eye for an eye, and a tooth for a tooth, and that it was lawful to hate one another, but as Christians, believing that "he who hateth his brother is a murderer." Ever do all that is consistent with honor to preserve this happy feeling.

Continue also to take the same lively interest in the moral and mental education of your dear children, who are so dear to my heart. Let your school be always as it is now, more than ever the model school of the Parish. Prove that you are sincere in your protestations of love for me by your fidelity in ever remembering and observing the many counsels you have received from me. "You are my friends if you do the things that I command you."

And now, my dearest friends, I must say to you Farewell, and may I request that you will ever ask for me in your pious prayers that which is my sole and highest ambition—to be a good priest. That the Giver of all good gifts may ever bestow upon you His choicest blessings and enable you so to live in this life that we may be together eternally happy in the next, is and ever shall be the constant prayer of your devoted friend and pastor.

E. J. DUNPHY, Priest.

Carleton, St. John, Oct. 26th, 1862.

The Address was read by Mr. Robert Rossiter, and the Reply given immediately after Mass on the last Sunday of Father Dunphy's sojourn in Carleton, and on all sides you could see the falling tears, or hear the more subdued sobs of the really grief stricken people, which burst forth into its intense bitterness when he bade them a sorrowful good bye, and for the last time raised his hands to invoke Heaven's choicest blessings on the people, from whom, at the call of duty, he so reluctantly parted. A couple of days after this sad and memorable scene a number of the most respectable and influential Protestant gentlemen of Carleton called on Father Dunphy and presented him with the following Address, as an expression of the feelings of the entire Protestant community :

ADDRESS TO THE REV. E. J. DUNPHY.

REV. AND DEAR SIR,—

Upon your retirement from Carleton, the scene of your labors for several years, the undersigned Justices of the Peace residing here would most respectfully address you.

Be assured, Reverend Sir, that it affords us great pleasure to be enabled to state that your truly Christian deportment, your excellent personal example and the moral persuasion that you have continually exercised have produced happy effects upon the conduct of those who have been directly under your charge. A result like this goes a long way towards elevating the character of a whole community.

Your influence, Reverend Sir, has ever been exercised in the promotion of good neighborhood and kindly feeling between man and man, and **be assurred** that you will be therefore long remembered **by the** undersigned and the inhabitants of **Carleton generally** with becoming regard.

May God prosper you in the promotion of **every** good **work.**

We remain, dear sir,

Very respectfully your obd'nt servants,

SAMUEL STRANGE, J. P.,	JAMES OLIVE, **3rd**, J. P.
JOSEPH BEATTY, "	JOHN C. LITTLEHALE, "
WM. C. DUNHAM, "	JOSIAH ADAMS, "
ROBERT SALTER, "	CHARLES KETCHUM, "
JOSEPH CORAM, "	SAMUEL CLARK, "

PETER STUBBS, Secretary.

The Reverend gentleman gave the following

REPLY.

Gentlemen,—

The compliment you pay me by the presentation **of this Address is one** I shall ever remember **with** pride and pleasure. As in duty bound, I have laboured to the best of **my humble abilities, aided by the** grace **of** God, to render my people good **Christians** and good citizens, and it is to me no small consolation to **be assured** that my labors have not **been** unsuccessful. Should they be happily followed by a beneficial effect on the whole community, I shall ever have reason to be thankful to

God. I am truly pleased to notice the good feeling now existing between all the Protestants of Carleton and my people. Knowing now the advantage of living together in peace and harmony, let us hope that nothing may ever occur to interrupt these kindly feelings. I am happy to have the opportunity of acknowledging the kindness and courtesy that have been invariably shown me by the Protestants of Carleton, and of them there are many whose attentions I shall never forget.

Thanking you for your kind wishes and assuring you of my sincere regards.

Believe me gentlemen,
Your very obedient servant,

E. J. DUNPHY.
Catholic Priest.

Carleton, Oct. 29th, 1862.

Father Dunphy sailed for St. Stephen on the 29th of October, and many a straining, tearful eye watched the steamer out of sight, and many heartfelt, earnest prayers went up to the throne of Heaven from saddened hearts, for the spiritual and temporal welfare of him who, though absent in person, would be ever present in the mind and hearts of many.

CHAPTER XVI.

REVEREND JAMES QUINN.

Father Quinn, of whom some mention was made in these pages at the commencement of these Memoirs, was the next resident priest in Carleton, and one who did much in the short time assigned him. Having been formerly in St. John, and while there occasionally in Carleton, his face was quite familiar to many of the older inhabitants. Time had dealt kindly with him, as he looked almost as hale and hearty as when he had departed for his former mission some ten years previous. I must be pardoned if I omit, or indeed what is more correct, disremember, the minor events connected with his short stay in Carleton, as I was absent three out of the five years he was in charge of the parish.

For some time the great want felt by the priest and people of Carleton was the absence of those religious teachers whose duty it is to impart to the children under their care, not only a secular but a good sound religious instruction or education, which special training not only fits them for this world but prepares them for the happiness of a better and more lasting one. To talk of introducing these " Religious " however, before preparing a suitable residence for their accommodation, was simply absurd, and as talk in such instances will absolutely effect nothing, the more important one of building was agitated by Father Quinn, which met with the hearty co-operation of the people. Collections were at once taken up for this purpose, and the contract for the work was accepted by Messrs. Wheaten and Fitzgerald. In a reasonably short time the house was completed, and now stands as a monument to this good priest's zeal and industry. It was in September following his departure for his second mission to St. Stephen that the good Sisters, four in number, with Sister Mary Teresa as Superioress, took possession of the new home prepared for them. During Father Quinn's mission in Carleton he also added a portion to the school house connecting with the old building, which gave increased facilities for the accommodation of the children wishing to attend school. The organ that now stands in the Church of the Assumption was also purchased by him from the proceeds of a pic-nic held during one of the summers he resided in Carleton. Such was the very valuable work done by Father Quinn during the five and a half years that intervened between his coming and departure from the parish, and in this, as in every instance of its kind, he had no doubt many difficulties to contend against.

CHAPTER XVII.

FATHER DUNPHY'S MISSION IN ST. STEPHEN—THE CHURCH AND PAROCHIAL RESIDENCE.

On the evening of the 29th of October, 1862, Father Dunphy arrived in St. Stephen. Here is a new sphere in which to begin the busy, active life, so characteristic of the man, so in accordance with that duty he so faithfully performed, no matter where situated, during his pastoral charge of twenty-seven years. The parish of St. Stephen is one of the very best in the diocese, not so much in regard to its numbers as to the comfort, if not wealth, of many, and the generous, benevolent and hospitable nature of the entire people. Father Dunphy left Carleton with many regrets it is true, but fortunate was it for him that when separated from the congregation he so loved, and for whom he so earnestly labored, that his future home should be in the midst of such a people. Kind at all times in a particular manner even to a stranger, paying them a social visit, it was nothing new or surprising that they welcomed him as their future pastor with a warmth and genuine heartiness that made him feel in a very short time perfectly at home. His first winter in his new parish glided quietly and happily by, becoming daily more and more familiar with the young and old, finding out the local habitation or business calling of each individual, and in every way uniting his interests as it were with theirs, so that by the following spring I question if there was a single person in his large parish that he could not name and at the same time refer you to his private residence or place of business.

The spring of 1863 finds the busy brain of Father Dunphy already maturing plans for the erection of a new Church. The existing one, it is true, cannot be removed from its old landmark, on the plea of want of room, for as I remember it, during my first visit to St. Stephen, it was large, roomy and sufficiently spacious for the congregation in attendance, but extremely old fashioned and entirely wanting in that internal or external beauty so pleasing to the eye, even in church architecture. No doubt many an old resident had a strong attachment to this sacred edifice, and many a pleasing happy memory in connection with it. Here, no doubt, many of them now in the autumn of life were washed in the regenerating waters of Baptism, here for the first time they knelt at those old altar rails to partake of the Bread of Life, and subsequently knelt in the flush of youth and happiness to receive that nuptial benediction which had no doubt aided many of them during many long eventful years, to bear and forbear, and by this means leading an honoured and respected life, true to each other and honestly, justly true to all with whom they came in contact. Here also some good, faithful and esteemed priests had laboured for the sanctification of their souls and the honor of God; and on many a Sabbath morning had they listened, within those honored and time worn walls, to the voice of their first pastor, the venerable Father Cummings, who for many years rested in the quiet churchyard of Milltown, within the very shadow of the first Catholic Church in the parish of St. Stephen, and which he attended so faithfully. His remains were removed some few years ago to the St. Stephen Cemetery, surrounded by many to whom he no doubt administered the first Sacraments. Here, also, the learned, eloquent and polished speaker, Father Wallace, labored for four years, when he was succeeded by Father Connolly, and eventually by

Father James Quinn, the successor of Father Dunphy in Carleton. With all these pleasing reminiscences of the past, the old building was nevertheless torn from its foundation, where it had withstood the heavy rains and violent storms of many a long year, and was replaced by a handsome, spacious building.

As you approach Milltown (a portion of the parish) from St. Stephen, the eye of the tourist is attracted by the handsome, well proportioned spire, which gracefully rears itself towards the ethereal blue of the Heavens, and on approaching a little nearer your vision is greeted and relieved with a full view of a handsome, well finished Church, nestling in as beautiful and picturesque a spot as you will perhaps find in the Province of New Brunswick. It is situated in the midst of a beautiful verdant and carefully tended lawn; and as you emerge from the Church the eye is naturally turned to the bright sparkling St. Croix, and the ear must necessarily take in the sounds of the swift rushing waters, as they laughingly leap from rock to rock in their maddening speed, to gain a more extended course. It is a stately and imposing structure and in every way a credit to the place and an honor to the Catholics of the community. The building is 104x66 feet. The height from the floor to the roof is 44, and to the top of the pinnacle 83 feet. It is erected in the Gothic style, and the plans for its erection were furnished by Mr. Stead, of Saint John. It is capable of comfortably seating about one thousand persons. The aisles are large, spacious and roomy, and the beautifully stained glass on either side, with those in front and rear, go to make up a Church which for beauty, finish and workmanship can hardly be excelled in the Province.

To the right as you enter is the priest's comfortable and cozy residence, in front of which is a neatly laid out and carefully tended flower garden, every thing in and around giving evidence of the refined taste of the occupant and the generosity of the people who so nobly responded to any calls made upon them in regard to their Church and its surroundings.

CHAPTER XVII.

THE SCHOOLS AND CHORAL SOCIETY OF ST. STEPHEN.

Independent of the material work accomplished by Father Dunphy during his short mission in Saint Stephen and vicinity, he did much to raise the intellectual and social standard of the good people, who for five and a half years were committed to his pastoral care. His first and most earnest attention, no matter where situated, seemed to centre in an especial manner in the children of the parish, and to their particular training of soul, heart and mind, he gave his undivided attention. To teach them the difference between right and wrong, and knowing the former to act fearlessly and independently, to instil into their young hearts a love for the true, the good and the beautiful, to be kind, generous and courteous to all with whom they came in contact, were lessons he never wearied of trying to impress on the minds and hearts of all, and many a young Saint Stephen child, now grown to manhood or womanhood, can look back with pleasure on those bright, happy days of their fortunate childhood, and in secret murmur a low, earnest prayer for him who, though now lying motionless and silent, taught them many salutary lessons, which must necessarily contribute much towards making them better sons and daughters, truer husbands and wives, happier, nobler fathers and mothers, an honor to their religion, and a credit to the community in which they happen to reside. To aid him in this good work he procured the services of some of the best teachers in the profession, and so successful were all in this noble undertaking that Father Dunphy had the reputation of having one of the best schools on either side of the Saint Croix. Previous to the close of these schools for the summer vacation a dramatic and musical exhibition was given, which would have done credit to older and more experienced pupils. At these entertainments, which were of a most pleasing character, were to be found the most influential and respectable portion of the Protestant and Catholic population, and by their presence and encouragement doing much to aid and strengthen a love for the good and beautiful in the children who were at no distant day to take their places as the future men and women of the community.

In connection with the good already effected through various means a Choral Society was organized for the musical instruction of those who had the desire or ability to perfect themselves in this very desirable accomplishment. The society had at one time a regular attendance of eighty members, who assembled once a week for instruction, and in a remarkably short time after its organization gave one of a series of Concerts, which was received with well merited applause by both press and public. The success of these Concerts, however, was mainly due to the energy, unremitting care and attention of their musical instructor, Mr. Bowers. Not only should the members of Saint Cecilia's Society kindly and gratefully remember this gentleman, but also the communities of Milltown and Saint

Stephen, for whom as a people he did much in awakening, fostering and disseminating a love for that musical culture which is so noticeable in many of the homes on either side of the Saint Croix.

CHAPTER XIX.

THE FIRST SAINT STEPHEN PIC NIC.

The beautiful Church of Milltown, of which I have endeavored to give an imperfect outline, could not be erected solely by the voluntary contributions of the people, no matter how generous or liberal they were with the means at their command. The success of their zealous priest in holding an annual Pic Nic, for Church purposes in Carleton, made him readily conceive the idea of adopting the same plan in his new field of labor. The suggestion was received with evident pleasure by his congregation, who willingly promised all and every assistance within their power, promises which the success of the affair readily proved, for where there is not union between even priest and people little if any good can be accomplished. The day appointed was Tuesday, the 28th day of August, 1863, and the beautiful grounds of Timothy Crocker,

Esq., the picturesque spot chosen for the holding of the first great social gathering of the Catholic communities of Milltown and St. Stephen. It is a charming place, situated two or three miles from St. Stephen, on what is known as the "Ledge Road," but sufficiently removed from the dust and its accompanying annoyances as to render the seclusion all the more inviting. To the right as you enter is what may be well termed Crocker's "Fairy Island," covered with a rich foliage, and here and there studded with trees, sufficiently ample to protect one from the burning rays of an oppressively hot mid summer sun. Opposite you flow the waters of the St. Croix, and on the other side of it one has a full and uninterrupted view of the lively, bustling and go-aheadative little American city of Calais. Visiting at the time among the hospitable people of whom I am writing, I early found myself ready to accompany my kind hostess to the scene of so much anticipated pleasure. As our spirited little animal sped with almost lightning rapidity over the dusty roads, we overtook the Sunday-school teachers and children, walking with uniform regularity, the bright eyes and happy, childish faces of the latter in keeping with their gay ribbons and neat holiday attire. Further on, as we emerged into the more populously settled portion of St. Stephen, the bustle and confusion, the almost entire suspension of business, gave one the impression that all were bent on enjoying the holiday with a zest and spirit that eventually benefits both mind and body. In a few minutes we find ourselves alighting at the entrance to the grounds, at which float quietly side by side the British and American flags. One of St. Stephen's wealthiest and most influential citizens is the first we meet, who does credit to himself and honor to the occasion by taking a share in the labors of the day. Immediately on entering, the sweet strains of the St. Stephen Cornet Band are heard in the distance, filling the air with the melody of its well-executed music. The loveliness of the mid-summer morning and the novelty of the affair had brought many even at an unusually early hour from the surrounding country, and one could not be otherwise than pleased to see the eagerness and vivacity with which so many, young and old, entered into the various amusements provided for their entertainment. The usual Pic Nic sports were being eagerly pursued by the assembled thousands, when music was heard in the distance, and on closer scrutiny the "Lion" was sighted, having on board a number of excursionists from St. John and Carleton, coming principally out of compliment to Father Dunphy, who was still warmly and gratefully remembered by many of the people from whom he had so reluctantly parted. Nearer and nearer came the steamer with her precious freight, and as she came opposite to the grounds one long shout of welcome issued from the assembled multitude on the shore, only to be returned with equal feeling and warmth by the somewhat wearied though much pleased excursionists. In a comparatively short time the tired travellers soon found themselves on terra firma, and immediately came the first great care, under nearly all circumstances of business or pleasure, the refreshing of the inner man. Ample choice was afforded them at the well laid and bountifully provided tables of the ladies in charge of this especial department and to which no doubt they did full justice after their tiresome and fatiguing journey. A cordial welcome was accorded to all from the warm, genial people whom they came to visit, and among whom for the first time they exchanged the minor courtesies of life, these simple attentions which on the part of many merged into a warm, strong friendship, which time, distance, or the vicissitudes of a chequered life cannot weaken, much less force asunder. Nearly three thousand persons were scattered over the ample grounds, all apparently well pleased and gratified, and still, through the care and energy of Father Dunphy, who seemed almost ubiquitous, everything was conducted with as much order and decorum as if this large and vast assemblage of all denominations and classes was but a small, well-regulated family. The sun had long set in the western horizon, ere the tired, though pleased and happy pleasure seekers, sought the sanctuary of their homes, many lingering even into the darkening twilight to talk over the pleasing events of the day, while the merry song and joyous laughter of hearts, young and untouched by care, made one feel how much happiness and genuine pleasure there is in the world, if the proper means are resorted to for the attaining of that after which all so persistently and naturally seek.

CHAPTER XX.

FATHER DUNPHY ON FENIANISM.

During the spring of 1867 the quiet of the border towns was disturbed by the appearance of a number of men who, on further investigation, proved to be the followers of Stephens the Fenian leader. The news spread with wonderful rapidity, and many silly and exaggerated stories were soon in circulation, frightening a few foolish enough to be imposed upon by the idle gossip of the many glad of a little excitement to while away an otherwise listless and idle hour. The men were on the whole quiet and inoffensive, but fearing the worst, Father Dunphy thought it well to refer to the matter, and on the Sunday following their arrival he delivered the following address to his congregation :—

"There is a certain subject upon which prudence required that I should be silent up to the present. Owing, however, to a certain event which has occurred during the past week the same prudence demands that I should speak, as my further silence may be misinterpreted, and myself and the Catholics of this town be thus placed in a false position. I refer to Fenianism, about which there has been so much needless excitement during the past few days.

"Whilst yielding to no man in the love which, as a native of Ireland, I bear my country; whilst deeply sympathizing with her in all those political grievances to which she is now and has been for many a century the unfortunate victim; and whilst believing that no one's life could be more nobly devoted than in redeeming his country's wrongs, I nevertheless cannot but scornfully condemn the wild scheme of the so-called Fenian brotherhood for the liberation of Ireland.

"At all times portions of mankind have been the victims of some mania or delusion, and I consider Fenianism a mania well worthy of the brain of a man who, if report speaks the truth, passed a portion of his life in a Lunatic Asylum. Owing to the ardent love of country which fills the hearts of Irishmen, they too often lend a willing ear to wild revolutionists who hold out projects for the independence of their country; they are too easily duped by the eloquence of the enthusiast or the cunning of the wily politician. But to any man not smitten with the mania, this must appear one of the most absurd and gigantic schemes of modern times. Were it not that Ireland is brought to shame and that Irishmen are humbled by the pranks of this mad man and his dupes, one might afford to laugh at them; but the affair, without becoming very serious, has lately assumed such inflated proportions that one is obliged to speak seriously of a thing which is in reality so silly. Ireland has grievances, many and weighty, which call loudly for redress; but her wisest and best men have no confidence in the success of revolutions. The fate of the revolutions in Hungary, Poland and the late Confederate States, is fresh in their memory, and they would, indeed, be deserving of all the folly attributed to them by their enemies did they not learn a lesson which the failure of these revolutions teaches. It is not by the shedding of blood Ireland has remedied, or hopes to remedy, her grievances. What did she gain by the revolution of 1798 or 1848? Less than nothing. These revolutions were miserable failures; they retarded the prosperity of Ireland, and that of '98 caused in a great measure the destruction of legislative independence. O'Connell and other wise statesmen have won Ireland more renown, and have redressed more of her grievances by their moral force doctrine, than any of the revolutionists that have figured during the present or past centuries, and whose names are now only remembered in connexion with the blood and banishment of many of her sons, who loved their country well but not wisely.

"The leaders of former revolutions in Ireland were men of splendid talents, and were for the most part men of irreproachable character; they commanded the respect of even their opponents; they won the sympathy of nearly all, and had the co-operation of a great body of other countrymen; but the Fenians excite only the derision or contempt of all sensible men, and have been almost universally censured by the Catholic clergy, the press and people of Ireland. Yet in the face of these facts, notwithstanding the failure of these revolutions, Fenianism is said to be widespread in the United

States and vast sums of money have been contributed to further its object. For our own and their sakes we must bitterly lament the reckless infatuation of our countrymen in the United States, who pretending to speak and act in the name of all Irishmen hold us up to the scorn of the ignorant and prejudiced. So far, however, from all Irishmen encouraging or sympathizing with the Fenians, I can safely aver in the name of my congregation and in my own—and many hundred priests could say the same—that we heartily condemn their project.

"You are doubtless aware that the Lieutenant Governor is reported to have said, at the recent meeting of the Magistrates of St. Stephen, that in the result of trouble arising from the Fenians there was no class upon whom he would more readily depend than upon the Irish Catholics of this Province. I trust you will show yourselves worthy of the confidence reposed in you, and that the young men of this congregation will vie with the other young men of the community in enrolling themselves in the volunteer companies which are about to be reorganized, and thus do your share in defending your homes and country against any raid that may be made upon them, though amongst the raiders may be found your own brothers.

"Though inclined to think that the Fenians have no serious intentions of trying to carry out their ostensible designs, yet as they have collected a great amount of money it is quite probable that they will make some show of spending part of it that they may be better able to pocket the remainder. They may make a raid on some of our frontier towns, causing some annoyance. They will then retire and say that nothing further can be accomplished until some further time. The leaders will then put the funds to their own private use, Fenianism will eventually die out and be forgotten.

"Be that as it may, it is our duty to prepare for the worst, and as we Irish Catholics have equal rights in this Province, as we enjoy all the privileges and blessings which a good government can afford, it becomes not only our duty but our dearest interests to defend our country against all and any aggressors.

CHAPTER XXI.

INTEMPERANCE IN MILLTOWN AND ST. STEPHEN.

The social evil of the sale and indulgence in strong drink Father Dunphy continually opposed, for in St. Stephen as in Carleton, and I may add nearly every habitable portion of the globe, this terrible evil too often creeps in to mar the peace and happiness of many for this world and endanger their salvation for the next and more lasting one.

To the entire extinction of this vice he put forth every effort—using here as elsewhere all available means within his power to stop the too frequent indulgence in intoxicating drinks, and with that success with which God seemed to bless his efforts in this direction, Milltown especially became a model town in this respect. St. Stephen to a certain extent reaped the rich reward vouchsafed to a portion of the parish, and to-day, both in Milltown and St. Stephen, are Temperance societies in a most flourishing condition, encouraged and presided over by that zealous **pioneer** Temperance advocate, Rev. James Quinn, **aided** in both places by members of the congregation noted **alike** for the zeal and untiring energy they display in the noble cause.

Much could be written in connection with **the** good people of St. **Stephen** and their zealous and esteemed priests, from the days of Father Cummings to their **present** venerable and justly respected **pastor**, Rev. James Quinn; but as these Memoirs relate particularly to the life of Father Dunphy, **I** must be pardoned if **I** more prominently bring his works before the public to the apparent exclusion **of** much **good** effected morally, socially **and** intellectually, by other faithful and zealous priests, who deserve the lasting gratitude and **affection of the people** over whom they **had or still have** control. Father Dunphy did **much** certainly for the people of St. Stephen, **by which he justly** earned that love and appreciation which **all** seemed willing **to** bestow on him in the many and successful efforts **made** in their regard, and at all times according him that **true,** genuine respect, **which** made **them** look **on this good** priest as **one who** not only brought **honor on** himself but **upon** the religion and people he so faithfully represented. Five and a half years were thus spent in the promotion of much good, morally, socially and **intellectually, when** Father Dunphy **was again summoned** to leave **the people** among whom he had labored with **so much** success, and to **whom in** time he became **sincerely** attached, through their unvarying **and** persistent kindness **and** the hearty cooperation so willingly and generously vouchsafed him in every undertaking **tending** to their spiritual or temporal advancement. The news of **his** intended departure was received with feelings **of the** most **genuine** sorrow and regret by all **denominations, and ere** his departure the following " **Address** " and " Resolutions " were presented to him, and **which I will** insert in these Memoirs in courtesy **to a people from** whom I received many kind **and** flattering **attentions** during the three **years** I was situated among them.

The following is the " Address," which was read by Patrick Curran, Esq.:

Reverend **and Dear Sir,—**

We learn with the most heartfelt regrets that you are soon to remove from amongst us. We feel this loss the more acutely as we hoped that you would long be with us as our pastor, to enjoy some of the fruits **of** your most arduous **labors in** the parish, and to carry out the improvements which are going on and the others which you had contemplated.

Enough has been done by you to entitle you to our warmest feelings of gratitude and love. To your enterprise and energy must chiefly be attributed the erection of the elegant and **spacious** Church, which was so **much** required for the **comfort of** the congregation **and the** respectability **of religion,** as **well as** the remarkable progress which has been made by our **community during the** past few years. The fact, moreover, that our Church and the extensive improvements of our **parochial** house are paid **for, and** that the parish is free from **debt,** reflects **the** highest honor on your business talent. Though **the amount** realized **for** Church purposes—about $23,000—appears **large, yet it is a** matter of surprise **how much** has been done **for that money, and in the** collection **of this sum no one** has **become the poorer, whilst we** believe that **God has abundantly blessed the cheerful giver. We** have the **satisfaction moreover of knowing that our Church** and parochial **improvements will long** exist **for the** benefit **of** ourselves as **well as of our children.**

We gratefully acknowledge **the services which you have rendered in** your zeal **in sustaining good schools for the education of the** rising **generation. Your own leisure time has ever been** devoted to **the spiritual and** intellectual **culture of the younger portion of our** community, and you must be consoled with **the** reflection **that they** have advanced in **those** tastes, accomplishments and **virtues** which will make them useful and honorable members **of society.**

Not only **they but all have** experienced the good results of **your** influence **in the** cause **of** morality and practical religion. We find that habits **of** self-respect, industry, sobriety, love of order and observance **of public law are now almost** generally prevailing amongst **the** members **of our** congregation. Whilst zealously working **for the** good **of** others your own **character** has been such **as to win** the esteem of all denominations, and through **you to bring** respect to the Catholic body in this parish.

When **to** these services **of a** public nature we add the very many proofs of the most sincere friendship which we have received from you we feel under the most lasting obligations, and as an expression of our thanks we respectfully present you with the accompanying purse of $466.00.

We now, Reverend and dear Father, bid you a sad farewell, but we hope to be with you in communion of prayer. Your name and good works will be fondly cherished in our memories, and we will pray that God will bestow upon you his choicest blessings, and that we will have the felicity of meeting you in that brighter, better, happier life, where the pain of parting from those we love shall be no more.

Signed on behalf of the congregation.

Hugh Cullinan,	John Short,
Patrick Cullinan,	George Fitzsimmons,
Patrick Curran,	Michael Daley,
Charles Short,	Daniel McDonald,
James Crangle,	Morris Daley,
Hugh Temple,	John McGarrigle.

REPLY.

My Very Dear Friends,—

The love of a Catholic for his priest is proverbial, and on many occasions, during the past five years, have you offered me abundant proofs of yours, yet I was not prepared to witness the very affecting manifestation of endearment which you and those dear friends whose sentiments you express have shown me since I informed you of my contemplated removal to another sphere of labor. To the reflecting Catholic this devotion to his priest is intelligible, for he well understands all that he and society owe to the ministry of the priesthood,—he well knows that the entire life of a Catholic priest is a long and heroic devotion to the spiritual and temporal welfare of those confided to his charge, a constant sacrifice of domestic joys, all the gratifications and pleasures which men so greedily seek after, for obscure duties and painful labors, the practice of which, while it consoles, wastes the heart. The Catholic considers his priest as his consoler by profession in the midst of all the cares and miseries attending humanity, his sympathizer in his sufferings: a guide and teacher whose words fall from on high upon the mind and heart with the authority of a divine mission. Therefore it is that he loves his priest, knowing how well he is loved by him. Love thus begetting love. Hence that reciprocity of love which so much astonishes those who see this cannot understand. Let me assure you, my dear friends, that those recent tears and stifled sobs, which I have so painfully witnessed during the past few days, have not been unreciprocated, and that had I not a firm conviction that my removal to another and a larger sphere of labor is the work of Providence, I would yet withdraw the consent which was not required of me, but which I gave for God and in His name, and which I am persuaded will be blessed by Him, for when God tries us, by requiring submission to the orders of His Providence, in such things as give pain to our natural feelings, when He demands of us afflicting sacrifices we may always cast ourselves into the arms of His Providence with a perfect certainty that those trials and sacrifices are for His greater honor and glory and for our good.

In severing myself from you it is to me a great consolation and a holy pride to have been instrumental in erecting our beautiful Church—one worthy of so good a people, and to you it is an immense credit and tells wonderfully of your generosity and your zeal for your holy religion to have enabled me in so short a period to defray all the expenses attending this and other parochial improvements—to cancel the old debt upon your school house and thus leave you free of debt and something to the credit of your Church. To you it is also most consoling to have this lovely and spacious Church, of which you are so justly proud, wherein you often may adore your God and seek him in your fears or hopes;

where you may find the Divinity always present, and where you may altogether tell your weakness and miseries.

But, my dear friends, only a very small portion of a priest's duty is accomplished by erecting the material edifice. He, it is true, must build the altar of sacrifice, lay on the wood, prepare the victim, but you must, by the fervor of your piety, the purity of your morals, and the holiness of your lives, cause fire to descend from heaven to consume the victim, and thus, by honoring and worshipping your God, build up and complete your own spiritual edifice. A priest can only give you the body of religion, you must seize the spirit, and with it nourish your immortal souls, and thus secure your present and future happiness; for whatever may be the social condition of man, whether he be fortunate or miserable he may and can by observing the morality of the gospel obtain true happiness.

The education of your children has been to me the most anxious and responsible of my priestly duties, for upon their proper education depends to a great extent their present and future happiness, as well as the future social prosperity of this parish. My aim has been not merely to break down ignorance and afford them a more intellectual culture, whether scientific or religious, but what is far more necessary, to give them a good moral education—the culture of the heart. By educating a child's mind, we teach him how to think; but if we wish to teach him how to act, we must educate the heart and its will, and thus enable him to chain the busy demon of passion, and to force languid nature to act according to the high standard of Christian purity and natural justice. To refine their tastes, open their eyes to the love inspiring influences of all that is good and great and beautiful, to enrich their understanding with a knowledge of the sublime teachings of our holy religion, has been my constant aim. This task once accomplished there necessarily follows habits of self respect, industry, sobriety, love of order, and observance of public law. You, my dear friends, know the extent of my success: if not as great as I would wish it only proves the difficulty of the task.

The munificent donation, which you present me in your own name and the name of my dear people, I estimate as it deserves, but believe me, my dear friends, I prize much more highly the love which prompted such generosity. With it I shall purchase a gold chalice or some sacerdotal vestment, which will ever serve as a precious souvenir of your love and attachment.

With this expression of my feelings in reference to the several topics alluded to in your affectionate address, in conclusion I exhort you to live and breathe only for God, to have a sinner's awe and a child's love for your only true Father.

I thank you with my whole heart and bless you with my whole soul, and shall ever pray that you may so live that, though severed for a time, we may hereafter live together eternally with our God. Pray for me. May God bless you. Farewell.

E. J. DUNPHY.

He was also the recipient of the following Correspondence and Resolutions, which speak for themselves:—

MILLTOWN, St. Stephen, May 16, 1877.

To the REV. E. J. DUNPHY, Pastor of the Catholic Church, Milltown, St. Stephen:

My Dear Sir,—I have the pleasure to enclose you a copy of Resolutions unanimously passed by the members of Wilberforce Division, Sons of Temperance, at their last meeting, and to express to you the regrets of our Division that the Temperance cause in this place is to lose one of its ablest advocates.

The writer most heartily approves of that resolution, and would further personally add his own high respect for your fidelity and zeal, not only for the promotion of the cause of Temperance, but also of Education and general improvement, and every good moral work, by which our citizens have been all benefitted, and I feel sure that the feeling of regret will be universal throughout our community at your departure.

With my best wishes for your health and prosperity.

I am, Dear Sir,
Very Respectfully Yours,
SAMUEL DARLING, R. S.

Whereas, It is understood that the Rev. E. J. Dunphy, pastor of the Catholic Church in this place, is soon to exchange this for another field of labor; and

Whereas, It is eminently fit and proper that an organization like the Sons of Temperance should gratefully acknowledge the services of one who has been so effective a colaborer in the cause of temperance, sobriety and good order;

Therefore Resolved, That the thanks of Wilberforce Division, No. 3, S. of T., are hereby tendered to the retiring pastor, for his earnest, able and efficient labors in the cause of Temperance in this community;

And Further Resolved, That the Recording Scribe be requested to present to the Reverend gentleman a copy of these resolutions, and also to express to him the regret of this Division that our cause in this place is to lose one of its ablest advocates.

(Signed)   CHARLES F. TODD,   }
                       W. O. MERRIAM,   } Committee.
                       CHARLES BOURDMAN, }

REPLY.

MESSRS. C. F. TODD, W. O. MERRIAM AND C. BOURDMAN:

GENTLEMEN,—Representing as you do a very respectable and influential portion of this community, I feel highly complimented by the Resolutions passed by your Division and presented to me by your Recording Scribe, Samuel Darling, Esq.

Believing Intemperance to be a hideous sin, the chief cause of many other sins, and the prolific source of every misfortune, I have, as in duty bound, laboured with my whole heart and soul to suppress it, and I am very much consoled to know that never were the people of Milltown so temperate and orderly as they are at present.

Milltown may now claim to be a model town, for there are few if any towns of equal population that can boast as it can of not having even one tavern, licensed, or unlicensed, and whose inhabitants are so orderly and respectable.

Hoping that the good work may be continued, thanking you for your kind regrets, and assuring you that I shall ever feel a lively interest in the welfare and prosperity of Milltown,

I remain, gentlemen,
Very sincerely yours,
E. J. DUNPHY.

MILLTOWN, May 18th, 1867.

CHAPTER XXII.

A JUST TRIBUTE OF PRAISE TO FATHER DUNPHY FROM THE PRESS OF ST. STEPHEN.

Feeling, or rather fearing, that some may be inclined to look upon me in the light of an enthusiast, where the subject of these Memoirs is concerned, I will permit another to speak, and so allow an impartial public to judge for themselves. The following is taken from a St. Stephen paper, edited and under the entire control of a Protestant gentleman :—

"On the departure of Father Dunphy from our midst it is befitting that we should make some acknowledgment of the worth and services of a man, who performed so much in a brief space of time for the good of those with whom he was more intimately connected, and through them in no small degree benefitted the general public. Milltown is now a quiet, orderly, respectable place. Some time ago a band of rowdies and drunkards resided there, who kept the lives and property of respectable people in constant danger. They openly defied the law and the public authorities. Several of them formed a "chain gang," and generally on Saturday nights waylaid passers by, insulting and often badly treating them. They used to make excursions into St. Stephen and Calais, and when met there by kindred spirits, scenes of disorder and disgrace usually took place. When Mr. Dunphy came here they soon began to feel there was an anxious eye upon them. Those of them who nominally belonged to his congregation were not only admonished but threatened with the power and aroused vengeance of the law. He got the Magistrates and respectable portion of the community to repel by force till the 'chain gang' lost link by link and is now completely broken up. He not only preached but did that rare thing, practised. He not only asked others to work but he worked himself. Many a swaggering bully who would fight all creation at night quailed before him in the morning. With rowdyism the low rum shops of Milltown began to disappear, so that at this time not a place where liquor is to be sold now exists. The social change which these things have brought about are observable. Young men who spent their time in rioting and drinking are now sober, saving and orderly. Others now spend their evenings in procuring domestic comforts for their families, instead of lavishing them upon intoxicating drinks. To the efforts of Rev. Mr. Dunphy are due in a great measure the invaluable improvements thus briefly alluded to.

"The erection of the beautiful Church on the road leading from St. Stephen to Milltown is the work chiefly of his enterprise and energy. Though it looks well on the outside yet, on the inside it is far better. The stained glass windows, the chaste altar, and the fine carvings throughout the Church present an appearance which is the model of simple grandeur. How the means could be obtained to build and pay for such a Church is to many a source of much surprise, especially when we consider the circumstances of some of the people and the short time taken to accomplish the work. Not only is the Church, which is a credit to St. Stephen, a monument to the great zeal of Mr. Dunphy in the cause of religion, but many other things of no small importance. He has well earned the affections of the Catholic community, and the respect of all other denominations. He bears away from all we can learn the character of being a highly polished gentleman, the truest of friends, an indefatigable laborer in his vocation, a man of unusual ability, and one whose work lives after him."

Father Dunphy left St. Stephen, followed by the united prayers of his congregation and the kind, sincere wishes of his many Protestant friends, upon whom they looked as a good citizen and a public benefactor; one who having through his exertions in their midst did much to establish that peace and love for order, the want of which is so keenly felt, particularly in small communities. Nearly eleven years have elapsed since that time, but through the varying changes in the drama of life, the St. Stephen people have, no doubt, retained for their esteemed and much **loved** pastor feelings of the liveliest gratitude and affection, and that affection I am certain follows him beyond his mere earthly career, and will live in the memory of many when time will have dimmed less holier and happier recollections.

CHAPTER XXIII.

RETURN OF FATHER DUNPHY TO CARLETON AND THE SUBSEQUENT ERECTION OF OUR PRESENT BEAUTIFUL CHURCH OF THE ASSUMPTION.

Truly may it be said, "Strange are the ways of Providence." Who among the many that mourned the departure of Rev. E. J. Dunphy could have forseen that in a few short years he would return to the mission where he had, through the assistance of God, achieved so much, and where with the same Divine help and the co-operation of his generous congregation, he would complete the work undertaken by him when Catholicity was only in its infancy in Carleton. It was on the 24th of May, 1867, that the Reverend gentlemen returned from Saint Stephen and whose arrival once again to the well known scenes of his early labors, need I add, was warmly welcomed by many a loving Catholic heart. Five years of toil and labor had left its evident effects on the usually pale and somewhat emaciated face, but the desire to save souls and work in all things for the honor and glory of God, was as warm, sincere and fervent as the day on which he left his dear Alma Mater, and the pious instructors to whom, even after the lapse of many years, he would refer with evident feelings of pleasure and affection.

As might be expected little could be done during the first year after his return, as it generally takes the better portion of that time to become familiar with many things, which, in the natural course of events, undergo more or less change, as time quietly slips away. In the following spring, however, he conceived the idea of enlarging our little Church, as it was becoming too small for the requirements of the increasing congregation. For this purpose he went earnestly to work, and by appealing to his people he made them also feel that they too must be in earnest, by giving him their hearty co-operation in the work he had in contemplation. As no undertaking of that nature can be effected without pecuniary aid, this was the first and most weighty consideration, and in order that the burden might not fall too heavily on a few,—the few who are found in every congregation to give cheerfully and willingly for such a purpose,—he resorted to a novel plan it is true, but which subsequently proved the wisdom that dictated it. As there are in the parish several districts and wards, and in these districts and wards all the Catholics comprising the Catholic community of Carleton reside, two young ladies were appointed to the several places, and by calling on each family once in the month, for six months in the year, the handsome sum of $2,156 was realized, and this, with the proceeds of a pic nic during the summer, materially helped to defray the expenses of building the transept, which was commenced on the 2nd of May, 1868. In May of the ensuing year preparations were begun for remodelling and otherwise renovating the old portion of the Church, which was commenced by constructing a new roof over the old one, till gradually it disappeared piece by piece, until there was no vestige of the old roof remaining, and so with the steeple, which was completed in the same manner, rearing its lofty and fair proportions under the guidance of skilled and finished artisans, much to their discomfort and anxiety at times, as it was a very critical and hazardous undertaking. Thus was our present handsome Church built on the ruins of the old edifice, which now lives only in the memory of many a Catholic heart.

The Church of the Assumption as it now stands is pronounced by all who have seen it a really handsome building, and one of the most beautiful wooden structures in the Dominion. This Church, the plans of which were furnished by Mr. Stead of St. John, is built in the florid Gothic style, and in its every appointment there is nothing to offend the eye of the most critical. The building is 101 feet eight inches long. The sides are 28 feet high and the apex of the ceiling from the floor is 40 feet. The depth of the transept is 42 feet, and its breadth 62 feet three inches, and the breadth of the nave 25 feet. The tower is 16 feet square and 78 feet high. The new spire rises 75 feet above the tower and is surmounted and ornamented by a handsomely illuminated cross, nine feet high, whose brightness is daily reflected in the distance by the rays of the sun. As you enter for the first time, the attention is naturally drawn to the general pleasing appearance of the entire building, but eventually the eye wanders from the graceful curves of the beautifully moulded ceiling to the large and handsomely stained glass windows, bearing the name of each donor, and placed there in memory of some dear departed friend, or as gifts to the beautiful Church, which through their generosity they materially helped to beautify. On either side run galleries the entire length of the building, and supported by pillars so light and graceful that they harmonize with the entire appearance of the sacred edifice. The altar and tabernacle, with some few changes and additions, are the same as in the old Church, and Reuben's beautiful "Descent from the Cross," still retains its place, a souvenir, as it were, of Carleton's first Catholic Church. In the spring of 1876, Father Dunphy, anxious to finish the work commenced with so many misgivings, and desirous to complete the Church of the Assumption, procured the services of a first-class artist in the person of Mr. A. Pindekowsky, of New York, to paint, fresco, and otherwise ornament and beautify the interior of the building. It only requires a visit to the sacred edifice to be convinced of the success of the undertaking. The painting and frescoing of the Church was the last material work to which Father Dunphy gave his attention, and even this was characteristic of the man, for, though I may say slowly dying, even then it was a matter of wonder and surprise to many the amount of time and personal supervision he gave to this his last material work in the Church he loved so dearly, and of which, when completed, he and his people were so justly proud. The Church of the Assumption, as it now stands, cost the comparatively trifling sum of $19,000. I say *comparatively*, for were it not for the personal supervision of the one who had conceived and undertaken the work, together with the utmost economy in the expenditure of the money entrusted to his care, it is very evident to any one who is at all conversant with building, and the enormous outlays such architectural undertakings entail, that this Church must necessarily have cost considerably more than the amount named above. To the zeal, economy and excellent business tact of the Rev. E. J. Dunphy, coupled with the hearty co-operation and open-handed generosity of the people over whom he had control, may be attributed the erection of one of the most handsome and commodious wooden Churches in the Dominion of Canada. It was consecrated in August, 1871, by His Lordship Bishop Sweeny, assisted by Revd. Fathers Michaud, Wallace and Ouellet.

CHAPTER XXIV.

THE CARLETON CATHOLIC HALL.

In the spring following the completion of the Church, Father Dunphy contracted, by some almost unknown means, a very severe cold, which seemed unwilling to yield to the efforts of professional skill, and at length, by the advice of his physician, he was compelled to seek in a warmer and more genial latitude the relief that could not be tendered him here. He consequently left for New York on the 5th of May, 1872, followed by the prayers of his anxious and troubled flock for his speedy and perfect restoration to health and strength. God, it would seem, was pleased to hear the prayers of so many earnest, loving hearts, as, after a lapse of a few short weeks, he returned with renewed health and strength to the duties he so reluctantly set aside.

The active mind of Father Dunphy could not rest, particularly when he felt a want remained which could be filled or supplied by his earnest attention to the matter. His first thought, after his arrival, was the erection of a Hall,—the want of which he, as well as many others, keenly felt for a long time. This building was commenced in June, 1872, and finished in the early part of November of the same year. The contract for the building was taken by Mr. Purdy French, and cost the sum of $7,500. It was opened to the public on the 26th of November, 1872, by a musical and literary entertainment, given by several accomplished and talented ladies and gentlemen residing in St. John and Carleton, in a rich and varied programme, which drew together a large and delighted audience, and realized quite a handsome sum. During the winter months a series of entertainments were proposed and given by some kind volunteers from the city, assisted by some of the more talented members of the community. The entertainments—dramatic and musical—were in themselves really excellent, the people warmly appreciating the efforts of those who not only ministered to their amusement in breaking the dull monotony of many an otherwise long and dreary winter evening, but likewise aided them in a more substantial manner, by relieving them of a further financial drain on their humble resources. However, the object Father Dunphy had in proposing the erection of St. Patrick's Hall, was more laudable than the mere fact of giving a few evening entertainments in it during the winter. It was to have a room or hall in which he would be enabled to form a Temperance Society, and through its medium have lectures and meetings from time to time, and by this means of banding themselves together, to more firmly withstand, with God's assistance, the numerous evils that the indulgence in ardent spirits brings to so many otherwise quiet, comfortable, peaceful, happy hearths and homes. A meeting of the congregation was called on the evening of the second Sunday of December, 1872, when a Temperance Society was formed, receiving the name of "St. Patrick's Total Abstinence and

Benevolent Society." Father Dunphy was chosen President and Spiritual Director, while other members of the congregation, noted for their sobriety and many excellent qualities, were appointed to fill the other official positions in the society. After the election of officers the meeting (which was largely attended) was addressed by the Rev. Father Michaud and the late lamented Mr. John O'Brien, at that time the honoured and much respected President of the " New Brunswick Union." After the very eloquent remarks by these gentlemen, some one hundred persons stepped forward and were the first to be enrolled among the many sons of the noble cause of temperance. Lectures were delivered on subsequent Sunday evenings, by some learned and talented gentlemen, and after the conclusion of each lecture new members were added to the lists, until the number had increased to some six hundred members. This was certainly a gratifying result, and a grand triumph in that glorious cause which has been in so many cases the means of rescuing many an otherwise worthy and honourable man from a state of degradation and sin, to which the too frequent indulgence in intoxicating drinks had reduced him. From week to week, and from month to month, Father Dunphy maintained the same earnest, warm interest in the temperance cause. Privately and publicly did he exhort his hearers to the practice of that virtue of which he himself was so brilliant an example. Not satisfied that a portion of his congregation was temperate, he conceived the novel idea of administering the pledge to the large numbers assembled at each of the Masses on one bright Sabbath morning. Promptly was the call responded to, and it was a really edifying sight, a beautiful and sublime spectacle, to witness an entire congregation rise unanimously at the call of that priest whose first great care was the salvation of their immortal souls. Never to the last moment of his life did he relax his interest in the society so dear to his heart, and who can tell the countless numbers of of souls he helped to save, through this one source alone, for a happy eternity. How earnestly I am sure he would say "God prosper the noble cause," and which should also be the prayer of not only every sincere practical Catholic, but of every man who wishes to see good done to his fellow man.

CHAPTER XXV.

GLEBE HOUSE, UNION POINT SCHOOL HOUSE AND CEMETERY.

The next material work that claimed Father Dunphy's attention was the Glebe House. From the time of his taking possession of it in 1854, no improvements had been made, and as a consequence it was becoming a little the worse of the wear and tear of time. Many necessary improvements were added, together with a handsome verandah, making the Glebe House one of the most comfortable and commodious in the diocese. This work cost $1600.

The Union Point school house becoming too small for the requirements of the pupils of that district and the comfort of the teachers, steps were taken in the spring of 1875 to enlarge the building, which improvements were completed under the personal supervision of Father Dunphy, at an expenditure of $1,300. As it now stands it is large, airy and comfortable, capable of accommodating between one and two hundred children, another monument to the zeal and energy of our late lamented pastor in the cause of education.

About this time he also purchased from Henry McCullough, Esq., a tract of land, consisting of seventeen acres, for which he paid $1,500. This he intended for a cemetery, when the present one would become too crowded for further interments, showing Father Dunphy's interest in the future congregation of Carleton was directed not only to their spiritual but even occupied his attention in regard to the material order.

CHAPTER XXVI.

FATHER DUNPHY'S ILLNESS, PRIESTLY DUTIES AND SUBSEQUENT DEATH.

About this time, September 1874, Father Dunphy began to show signs of failing health. He had been a man, although of slender form, the fortunate possessor of a strong constitution; but his arduous and unceasing toil in building, in the pulpit and confessional, together with other various duties, were beginning to be perceptibly felt by him, and were making serious inroads upon his hitherto enduring physical organization. From the day of his ordination till the day of his death, his active mind never rested. His was indeed a busy life, entirely devoted to the spiritual and temporal interests of each individual member of his large congregation. None could escape his personal supervision, from the frail child of a few years to the aged and tottering man. He knew each and every one committed to his pastoral care, and by this means did he endeavour, in an especial manner, to attend to the spiritual wants of his children. How many times have I known him, after the manifold duties of Sunday were over, when others would naturally rest, to leave his quiet, comfortable home, for the purpose of hunting up some neglected father or mother, or which was to him in a certain sense worse, an erring son or daughter, for to the rising generation did he always look for the future men and women of the parish. I will here quote the language of the *Freeman* of the 26th of September: "Constantly working for the glory of God and the good of his flock; at Mass, in the confessional, on sick calls, in his schools, in which he never seemed tired of working; among the workmen employed upon his buildings; visiting all who were in trouble and required his aid; preaching, praying, exhorting, comforting, reproving; priest, schoolmaster, master workman, the depository of all the cares of his people, he worked incessantly and with a vigor of which so feeble a constitution seemed incapable.

"And so he laboured day and night, in season and out of season, never ceasing a moment, never thinking of himself, but ever occupied in the service of God and of his people, teaching them by words and example to live soberly and religiously, allowing none to perish through his neglect. The prevalent vice of drunkenness he constantly warred against, not merely by preaching and exhortation, but by personal and repeated appeals to the drunken father, the reckless mother, and the young man or woman entering on a career of folly. These, when necessary, he sought in their own homes or haunts, often coming on them by surprise, and using with them persuasion or authority as it seemed best."

Such was truly the life of Father Dunphy during his pastoral charge of nineteen years in Carleton. The first symptom of illness which seemed to claim his attention was his failing eyesight, as it was with difficulty he could manage to read after lamplight, and on more than one occasion he was compelled to wear glasses in order to read the evening paper. His eyes, however, soon became strong again, but with that returning strength he grew physically weaker. He finally called on Dr. Travers, in whom he had always the utmost confidence, who pronounced his disease beyond the reach of medical skill. Remedies were, however, administered and every effort made to fight against the insidious attacks of the foe. During the winter he was evidently losing a little all the time, but so gradually one could perceive but very little change in him from day to day. The very best physicians in the city of New York were consulted by letter, but apparently could do no more than those at home. So he continued during the long winter, never relaxing for a moment the many duties of his sacred calling. In the spring his more intimate friends tried to prevail on him to take a trip to New York, or some more genial climate, where he would escape the cold raw winds and uneven temperature of our late springs. But no amount of reasoning or persuasion could induce him to lay aside, even for a few short weeks, the onerous and manifold duties of his pastoral charge. In August of 1875, a retreat of the priests of the diocese was held at Memramcook, at which he was present, and we can well imagine the effort required on his part to attend the regular daily exercises in his weakened condition. Shortly after the retreat, a mission was given in St. John, Portland, and eventually in Carleton, which was attended by the happiest results. Father McGuire, the able, eloquent and truly noble Irish priest, will be long and kindly remembered in Carleton, as well as in the many places he visited during his saintly visit in New Brunswick. The mission closed in Carleton on the second Sunday in September, 1875, and on the Tuesday following, Father Dunphy, after the earnest entreaties of his many friends, left home for New York, followed by the fervent prayers of his anxious congregation. Arriving at the home of his brother, whose residence is in the great city of New York, he lost no time in calling on two of the most eminent physicians to be met with in that modern Gotham. He was assured by them that he was in the first stage of consumption, and that his restoration to health was impossible. Calmly and patiently resigned to the will of God did he receive this announcement, which, to others more wrapped up in worldly matters, would have been intelligence of the saddest kind. Still, while he remained in New York, he seemed to improve a little, and on the whole he returned, after four weeks absence, somewhat better than was anticipated. Again he took upon himself the usual pastoral cares of his every day life, and no matter how weak or exhausted he might have been, he would leave no duty unfulfilled. At length, seeing that each day he was growing weaker and more emaciated, Bishop Sweeny insisted upon sending some one who would relieve him of many duties, and give him an opportunity of resting somewhat from the innumerable cares incidental to a large parish. Father Walsh was accordingly sent and celebrated his first Mass in Carleton on Ash-Wednesday. He felt the benefit arising from Father Walsh's willing assistance, and seemed to rally somewhat for a short time. It was in April, 1876, he contracted with Mr. Pindekowsky for the painting of the interior of the Church, and his almost constant supervision, during the progress of this work, materially helped to weaken him. The weather was wet and disagreeable at the time, and, as might be expected, his cough became daily more and more severe. Towards the first of June, the Church being nearly completed, he reluctantly left a second time for New York, in company with his brother. Finding the heat too oppressive at the time to be either pleasant or agreeable, through the advice of his physicians and friends he left for Lake George. In one of his letters home he thus speaks of it:—

"You see, by the heading of this letter, that I have changed my location. I found that while in New York I was rather losing than gaining; I felt the necessity of some change, and on Friday last, after a very fatiguing journey by steamer, rail and stage coach, I arrived here, at the most beautiful Lake in America—Lake George. It is truly beautiful, and is the resort of many in search of health, pleasure or repose. The Lake is about thirty-six miles long, by from one to four wide. In places it is three miles deep and so clear is the water that objects can be seen at a great depth. It is three hundred and thirty feet above the level of the sea, and one hundred and **forty above** Lake Champlain, and nestling among green mountain ranges from one hundred to two hundred feet high. The shore and mountain sides are studded with hotels, wonderful for their size and gorgeousness, with wealthy private residences, and the lake dotted with verdant islands—it is truly magnificent. Moreover, the surrounding **country** is full of reminiscences **of the** wars a century and **a half ago,** between **the** French and English, and of the **old** revolutionary wars between Americans and English, with a sprinkling of Indians on both sides. Relics gathered through many years from fort **and** battle-field, from **the** forest and from the bottom **of** the lake ; **rude** implements **of Indian** home life and **savage** warfare are to **be seen in** many of **the** hotels and **some** private houses of Lake George. Had I **but** the vigor **of a few** years ago, there would be few of those **old** forts, battle-fields and other objects of interest that I would leave unexplored. Directly opposite to my **hotel is a** mountain of one hundred and seventy-five feet high, on the very peak of which is 'Prospect Hotel,' from which I need not say there must be a magnificent view. Oh ! that I had the vim of old ; had I, I would have ere this enjoyed a sight never to be forgotten. But now I am—"

Here he abruptly breaks off, losing sight as it were of the beautiful in nature, to indulge in those feelings peculiar to one **in** an enfeebled state of health, particularly when shut out from home **and friends. It was** during his sojourn at Lake George that the members of the Catholic Total **A**bstinence **Union of New** Brunswick held **their** fifth annual **convention in** St. Patrick's hall. **At** the previous convention, in St. John in 1875**, it** was proposed and unanimously carried that, out of compliment to Father Dunphy, who had accomplished so much in regard to the Temperance movement, the following convention should be held in Carleton, which was accordingly carried into effect on the 29th and 30th of June, 1876. It was no doubt with much regret the delegates from the various societies learned, on their arrival, of the unavoidable absence of the honored President of St. Patrick's society. Though far away in body, in mind, spirit, and desire, he was with them in every thought or resolution that tended to the advancement of the cause he had always so near at heart. On resuming business after dinner, and when all were engaged in the various duties assigned them, a letter was received from Father Dunphy, and, on motion of the President, all arose from their seats, out of respect to the man who, though many miles distant, was with them in heart and soul. Amid breathless silence the letter was read, which I will insert here for the benefit of many interested, and which was kindly supplied me by the energetic and obliging President of the New Brunswick Union, R. J. Ritchie, Esq.:

Fort George Hotel, Lake George,
New York State, June 25th, 1875.

Mr. President and Gentlemen,—

Last year, when I proposed that Carleton should be favoured and I honored by having the next convention held in my parish, I no doubt would have denied myself the favor and the honor had I even thought I should be deprived of the very great privilege and pleasure of being an humble colaborer with you, Mr. President and gentleman, in a cause ever dear to me, because I believe it to be very dear to God, a powerful auxiliary in promoting all men's, but especially our own poor men's, comfort and happiness, propagating our Holy Faith and advancing God's honor and glory.

I very much regret that illness compels me to be where I now am, yet though far removed from the scene of your labors, I truly welcome you to my parish. I shall be with you with my whole heart and soul, and I shall pray God to inspire you with wisdom and direct all your thoughts and words to the one and sole object for which you are convened, viz.: the promotion of Temperance through the instrumentality of the New Brunswick Total Abstinence Union.

Believe me, Mr. President and gentlemen, very sincerely and respectfully yours,

E. J. DUNPHY.

After a sojourn of a few weeks at the Lake he returned to New York, and after resting sufficiently he again bade adieu to his friends, which proved a last farewell, reaching home on the 6th of July. Little change for the better was noticeable in him by the many anxious friends who called to see him after his return. Day after day he appeared to grow weaker and more emaciated, but still never relaxing a single remedy that he thought would be of service to him. Many duties even in this weakened condition were cheerfully attended to, the strong will and determined spirit of the man asserting themselves over the weaker physical powers. The sacrament of Confirmation was soon to take place in his Church, and you could see the interest of old awakened in regard to the most trifling details. The excitement seemed to have a beneficial effect on him, for though unable to go to the Church on the Sunday on which the ceremony took place, he seemed to take a lively interest in all that was going forward, and at dinner he sat at the table with His Lordship and the accompanying priests. On Monday he seemed to retain the same spirit and strength of the two previous days, but on the following day a reaction took place and a complete prostration was evident. He continued to sink perceptibly till about three o'clock on Saturday afternoon, when he complained of a violent pain, as he thought, about the heart. Always patient and quiet his suppressed moaning was distressing to those compelled to witness his intense suffering, without being able to alleviate his misery. Remedies were applied, and after an hour or so he became better. Towards six o'clock he was removed from the drawing room to the parlor, and after a few moments expressed a desire of retiring. Immediately after his removal to bed the pain again returned, and after a time vanished as in the afternoon. He became quieter, for a time, resting as well as could be expected, with intervals of coughing and fever, till three o'clock, when an evident change took place. His faithful attendant seeing that death was rapidly approaching, immediately called Father

Walsh and his nephew, Mr. E. J. Dunphy, who had arrived from New York on the previous Tuesday evening. He seemed perfectly conscious, and at four a. m. despatched a messenger for Dr. Travers, with the hope that he could relieve him of the pain from which he continued to suffer. Before the doctor's arrival, all that was mortal of Father Dunphy lay quietly at rest, and the immortal spirit of a great and good man had winged its flight into that unknown world, where the soul for the first time beholds the awful majesty of its Creator. Father Walsh administered the last sacraments, and in a few short moments after he quietly resigned his pure soul into the hands of that God whom he had taught thousands to love and revere. Yes, as quietly and as calmly as the frail, helpless infant, did he pass from the manifold cares of this life into the portals of eternity, there to receive the reward of his long and faithful stewardship.

Immediately was the Church bell slowly and solemnly tolled, wafting on the silent air of that sad Sabbath morning, the melancholy news to his many orphaned children and innumerable friends, that the kind father and affectionate friend was no more, that the active spirit at last rested, and the soul of one whom they so much loved and honored had passed to the bosom of its God. The sad news fell on all like a funeral pall, casting gloom and sadness into every home in Carleton and vicinity. Many were the low, murmured, earnest prayers wafted to the Throne of Mercy from many a crushed and broken heart, for the eternal repose of him who, on many a previous Sabbath morning, had taught them how to live, and by so living be prepared to die.

At the end of the solemn tolling of the bell, one of his faithful children composed the following beautifully expressive lines, and which were dedicated to his memory :

> Slow swings the bell, and solemn comes the knelling
>   Upon this Sabbath day,
> To weeping friends and saddened bosoms telling
>   A soul has passed away.
>
> Telling in saddest tones each struggling spirit,
>   Its dark and heavy loss,
> That he is gone, gone for his crown of merit,
>   Our soldier of the Cross.
>
> Telling the poor that hand that fed their hunger
>   And clothed them from the snow,
> That angel hand will minister no longer,
>   Our friend lies cold and low.
>
> Telling in many a home where zealous burning,
>   He crushed the Serpent's head,
> That meek eyed Temperance this day is mourning,
>   Her great apostle's dead.
>
> God's will be done—nor judge by human scope,
>   The bell has changed its tone,
> Our grief ascends upon the wings of hope,
>   Up to God's mighty throne.

> Where late the white-robed, angel ceased to sing,
>   The brief command was given,
> Then smiling flew down to earth, **to bring**
>   A saintly soul to Heaven.

After his death he was robed for the last time in the vestments he loved so well, and in which he so often celebrated, with love and reverence, the Holy Sacrifice of the Mass. This sad duty was ended a few moments previous to the departure of the congregation from early Mass. At this and the second service, Father Walsh, after recommending the soul of their deceased pastor to their earnest prayers, spoke in feeling and appropriate terms of their good priest, who had that morning been summoned to the judgment seat of God, to render an account not only for his own soul, but for each soul entrusted to his watchful care. Amidst the falling tears of the large congregation did he refer to the spiritual and material work accomplished for them by the dear one now lying cold and low in death's icy and relentless clasp. After the conclusion of each service, his body, which had been laid in the drawing room, and which he had so often graced with his agreeable conversation and gentlemanly demeanor during life, was visited by hundreds of his sorrow stricken children. In the afternoon, and during the following days till Tuesday at ten o'clock, his remains were visited by hundreds of all denominations from St. John, Portland and many outside places. Owing to the unusual warmth of the atmosphere and the continual and unceasing flow of visitors, it became necessary for those in attendance to reluctantly close the doors, necessarily preventing many from taking a last sad look at one upon whom in life they had ever loved and esteemed. It was hard, indeed, almost cruel, to refuse the piteous appeals of some poor creatures who had come a distance to have, as they expressed it, one last look at him who in life had been so kind a father to their helpless little ones. One poor woman, after having travelled a distance of fifty miles, when told it was impossible to see him, for in allowing her the same favor should be extended to the many at that moment pleading for admission, she burst into a violent paroxysm of grief, telling, through her falling tears and broken sobs, what he did for her and her five orphan children, fifteen years previous. What could be done with the poor sorrow-stricken creature? A few flowers from his casket were at length offered her as the only amends within reach to soothe the violent grief of the truly widowed heart. With what eager gratitude she accepted the lowly offering, and, kissing them with most affectionate reverence, placed them beneath the folds of her scanty black shawl. In the evening his brother, accompanied by his estimable wife, arrived from New York, and were much effected by the sad sight before them. That kindly eye was now closed forever; that earnest, pleading tongue was motionless; that large and generous heart had ceased to throb and was paralyzed in death. Yes, the voice that would have welcomed them to his home was hushed and silent, and the hands that would have been extended to them in the warm clasp of a kind, brotherly welcome, all was insensible to their presence and lay before them pale, mute and motionless. During the long and silent watches of the night mourners lingered lovingly by the remains, ever and anon thinking that in a few short, fleeting hours, Father Dunphy would be taken for the last time from the home that twenty-two years previous he had entered full of life and hope for the future. With a burning zeal for the honor of God and the welfare of his people, did he enter on his mission, and there, lying motionless and quiet, who could say that every duty had not been faithfully and conscientiously fulfilled. Six o'clock on Wednesday morning, September 27th, was the hour appointed for the remains to be taken from his residence to the Church,—that Church he loved so well. Slowly breaks the gray dawn of that eventful morning, and already you see the early mourners wending their way to the Church, or loitering around the garden and adjoining grounds. A few minutes of the appointed time, and six of his faithful parishioners lift from their last resting place the remains of their worthy and beloved pastor. Everything seems in keeping with the sad and melancholy scene. The dreary gray and leaden sky of that September morning— the dying, fading flowers and falling leaves, with the low sad murmur of the wind moaning as if in pity and in sorrow through the almost leafless trees, chiming, as it were, in unison with the overcharged sorrowing hearts of his numerous congregation. Slowly moves the funeral cortege from the house, preceded by the Carleton Serenade Band, playing in saddened tones the music of the Dead March. Then come the white-robed priests and attendants, followed by the casket on which are placed a handsome floral cross and many choice rare flowers, last tributes of love and affection from his many friends. The Requiem Mass was announced for nine o'clock, and long before that hour the beautiful Church of the Assumption was filled to its utmost capacity. All classes and denominations were assembled within its spacious walls, anxious to pay the last sad tribute to the memory of the man whom all alike respected. Conspicuous among the vast assemblage were the Protestant clergymen of Carleton and the gentlemen forming the Board of School

Trustees of the city of St. John. Willing hearts and hands had draped the entire Church in black,—fit emblem of the mourning of many saddened hearts. The casket was raised to an appropriate height, and on either side was surrounded by fourteen little girls, arrayed in white, with mourning badges. All was still and solemn, the large congregation was hushed to the deepest silence, when his Lordship, Bishop Sweeny, together with the white-robed priests and attendants, entered the sanctuary, many of them coming from quite a distance to do honor to the remains of their dear brother in Christ. As they entered one noticed the familiar face of Rev. James Quinn, St. Stephen; Rev. F. X. J. Michaud, Rev. A. Ouellet, Rev. Joseph Murray, Rev. James McDevitt, of St. John; Rev. William Foley, of St. Andrews; Rev. J. Vereker, of Sussex; Rev. Edward Doyle, of St. George; Rev. Father Precilius, of Fredericton; Rev. P. Farrell, of Petersville, and Rev. Thomas Walsh, of Carleton. The Requiem Mass was celebrated by Father Doyle, with Father Murray as Deacon, and Father McDevitt as Sub-Deacon. Towards the close of Mass, Father Michaud ascended the altar and preached the funeral sermon, taking for his text:

" And all the people of Israel bewailed him with great lamentations, and mourned for him many days and said : 'How is the mighty man fallen that saved the people of Israel.' "—Words taken from Mach 1, 9.

Dear Brethren,—

How sad and sorrowful is the duty we are assembled to perform on this day. The Church mourns for the death of one of her most zealous and faithful priests; we have lost a dear brother, a kind friend; you, bereaved people, lament the sudden though not unexpected departure of a beloved and devoted father. Desolate parish, you have lost the good shepherd who, for nearly a quarter of a century, fed you as the lambs and sheep entrusted to his care by Divine Providence; you have lost the good pastor who devoted himself entirely to the salvation of your immortal souls; you have lost a father who preached more to you by example than by words. In the language of Saint Paul to the Corinthians he addresses you to-day from the tomb these parting words: 'You know that serving the Lord with humility and tears, how I have kept nothing back that was profitable to you, but I have preached to you and taught you publicly, and from house to house, testifying penance towards God and faith in our Lord Jesus Christ. And now, behold, I know that all you, amongst whom I have gone preaching the kingdom of God, shall see my face no more." O! what a painful separation; what a sad farewell. May God give us, as he gave to the inconsolable people of Corinth, the strength to bear it with resignation. But, bereaved flock, surrounding the remains of your dear pastor, you are called upon to day to perform a duty of faith, a duty of love, a duty of gratitude. You are here to-day to pay a tribute of strict justice, as well as of piety and religion, to one who for so many years was responsible for your souls, and who, at the moment of his death, had not only to account for himself, but for each and every one of you as the flock entrusted to his pastoral care and solicitude. You are called to attest your love, by your ardent prayers and supplications to Heaven your gratitude, your veneration and undying affection to one, who, having by the gospel begotten you to Jesus Christ loved you so well;

who loved you as only the Catholic Shepherd of the true fold of Christ loves his little ones; who bore all things, hoped all things, and endured all things for your sake, and who, like St. Paul, would gladly be anathema all his life, in order to win you and secure you for the Heavenly fold above. As your beloved pastor loved you, and was faithful to you, and devoted to you to the end, so be it said to your honor that you have been faithful to him, and devoted to him and loyal to him in life and death. What the people of Corinth were to St. Paul, be you to your beloved and much regretted father. What is his living epistle, his certificate of character, his best letter of recommendation to God and men? Now, bowing down before the Will of the Most High, who called unto Himself the holy priest, whom he had lent you for a time, make a generous sacrifice, and in your deep affliction submit, without a murmur, to the inscrutable designs of Divine Providence. A good and zealous priest is the greatest blessing that Heaven can bestow on a parish. May you then, by your fidelity in corresponding with the grace of God, continue to deserve in future the same favor. Though death has struck down your lamented pastor, as it were before his time, and torn him momentarily from your view, yet, in point of fact, he is not dead: he was only fatigued and worn out with his labors. As the Good Shepherd he consumed his life for his flock. God said it was enough and gave him a sweet repose. His body is now at rest; it is but slumbering until the Archangel's trumpet shall summon him and us. Yes, like the great Apostle, he has fought the good fight; he has finished his course; he has kept the faith; and, as to the rest, there is laid up for him a crown of justice which the Lord shall render to him at that day. Yes, though he is now in the midst of the shadow of death, he shall fear no evil, for God is with him,—" for if any one will keep my words," says the Lord, "he shall not die forever, and he shall be in everlasting remembrance." O God hear our fervent prayers; look upon thy servant with mercy; reward his works; crown his virtues; give him eternal rest. Him—who raised to Thy honor and glory a temple so beautiful and so worthy, but which is only a feeble temple of his soul, which he adorned by all Christian virtues,—receive in thy kingdom; give him place among thy saints and angels.

Dear people, treasure up the sainted memory of your departed pastor. Often bring to mind the sacred maxims and glorious Gospel truths which he so forcibly inculcated; meditate on his life; imitate his virtues; recount all the grand points of his character to your children, for he was endowed with virtues which make men really just before God and before the world, and which are the foundation of that glorious immortality to which we aspire.

Yes, Father Dunphy was a holy priest, an honor to religion and an ornament to society. He was a saint according to God's own heart, and this is the title which endeared him to all who knew him. How zealous and persevering he was in every thing tending to promote the glory of God, the honor of religion and the good of his people. As much as he loved virtue and practiced it so much did he hate vice and shunned it. How faithfully did he watch over his dear flock, whose welfare, both spiritual and temporal, was the whole object of his thought and ambition; with what assiduity did he teach you the saving principles of religion; with what solicitude did he prevent his children erring from the path of duty and virtue; and with what zeal did he bring back to the fold the stray sheep wandering from their God. What charity for the poor, the sick and the afflicted, who always found in him a consoler, a friend, a father; what purity and simplicity of life, delicacy of conscience and exactitude in the performance of all his religious duties; what tender devotion and dignity in the holy functions of his ministry. In a word, dear people, you know how much he loved God and you; how dear you were to his heart; because you were dear to the heart of Jesus. His works are there as a monument testifying his merits before God and **men.** Therefore let his memory be **in** everlasting veneration amongst you, for he will, we trust, **be for** ever more the tutelary Angel of this parish; he **will be forever** standing at the golden altar before the throne of God, offering up your prayers and his own that you may be united with him in that Heavenly fold where Jesus is the everlasting Shepherd, and where, in his own **words, we are** never to be separated again.

Dear people, the end, the hope and the object **of** all our desires, as Christians, should be the possession **of** Heaven, for "**what does it profit a** man to gain the whole **world if** he loses his own **soul.**" **Let** us meditate on the awful lessons of death. Time **is short; life is** uncertain; we are but exiles in this **valley of tears and** sorrow. Heaven is our country, **our home.** Let us prepare, therefore, to meet our God, or rather, like **the** model we have before us, let **us** be always ready. **With** confidence in the mercies of God, **let** us fulfil our glorious destination, and thus we shall be entitled to a share in the fruits of Redemption, and instead of dying the death at the close of our mortal pilgrimage, we shall enter with Christ's true disciples into life everlasting. AMEN.

A warm personal **friend of** the deceased, the preacher could well **do justice** to the subject of his remarks. Warmly, **lovingly, did** he portray **the** character **of** the **dead father,** lying for the last time in view of **his** many orphaned children. Truly did he dwell **on all the** sacrifices **made by** the good shepherd **for the flock** entrusted to **his** care; to his many public and **private** virtues; **to** his warm, fervent zeal in the **cause** of religi**on,** and all that tended, directly or indirectly, to the spiritual wants of the many dear children committed to his pastoral care, and above all his purity of life and the honor his spotless and unblemished reputation cast as it were on the sacred calling of the priesthood.

His Lordship Bishop Sweeny then read the funeral service, after which the Temperance society, which had attended in full mourning regalia quietly left the Church to await the removal of the remains to their final resting place. The casket was lowered for removal, a procession followed from the Church to the Sacristy, consisting of the priests and their attendants, with the immediate relatives of the deceased; and none in that vast assemblage mourned him more sincerely than the faithful housekeeper, who for twenty-two years had attended to his every want. The Sacristy is reached, the handsome casket is enclosed in one of lighter material, the precious weight is lowered, amid the tears and sobs of the assembled thousands, and, in a few short moments, all that is mortal of Rev. E. J. Dunphy is forever closed from sight.

What more kind, and let me hope, indulgent reader, can I write. The task I undertook, with so many misgivings, (if task I can call it) is finished.

Nearly, as I possibly could, have I related the eventful, busy career and the work accomplished by Father Dunphy, particularly in Carleton, from the time he crossed the blue waves of the broad Atlantic, till he was lowered into the gloomy vault beneath his Church, personally superintended by himself two years previous. Passing away at the comparatively early age of fifty-three, he " sleeps the sleep that knows no waking," far away from the land of his birth, but among the people for whom he labored so earnestly for so many years, and for whom he entertained nothing but feelings of the most fatherly love and tenderness. " He is not dead but sleepeth." The frail mortal body lies mute and motionless within the confines of its narrow grave, there to await the sound of the great Archangel's trumpet; and, while sorrowing for the loss of our beloved pastor, let us mingle with our sorrow the blessed hope that his pure spirit rests in our only true home—Heaven; and where, before the throne of the Mighty One, he will offer incessant prayer in behalf of the many dear children he left to mourn him in this fleeting, transient world of ours.

Requiescat in Pace.

www.ingramcontent.com/pod-product-compliance
Lightning Source LLC
Chambersburg PA
CBHW022139160426
43197CB00009B/1353